The Call of Katahdin

Life in Werler's Woods

Best Regards

Werler
11/15-03

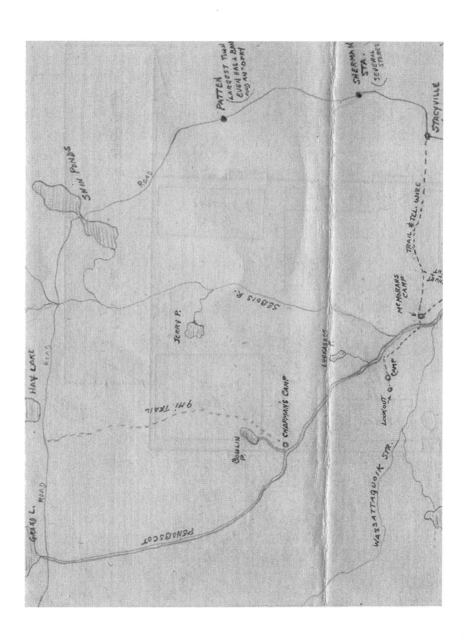

II

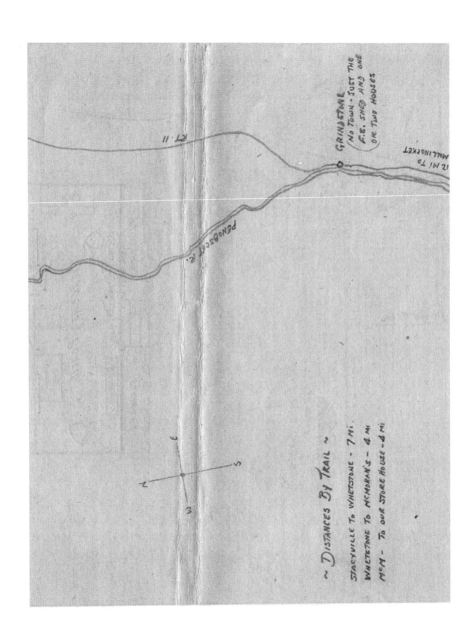

RT. 11

GRINDSTONE
(NO TOWN - JUST THE
F.S. SHED AND ONE
OR TWO HOUSES)

12 MI TO
MILLINOCKET

PENOBSCT R.

PENOBSCOT R.

~ DISTANCES BY TRAIL ~

STACYVILLE TO WHETSTONE - 7 MI.

WHETSTONE TO MCMORAN'S - 4 MI.

MCM - TO OUR STORE HOUSE - 4 MI.

III

The Call of Katahdin
Life in Werler's Woods

Ed Werler

Book design
Suzanne Almy Brown

Cranberry Knoll Publishers LLC

ISBN: 0-9614737-2-X
Library of Congress Catalog Number: 2003113302
First Printing,November, 2003
Printed in the United States of America
Cranberry Knoll Publishers LLC, Yarmouth, Maine 04096

Dedication

I started writing this book in 1995 wanting to pass on to my children Eddie and Cathy the story of how their mother and I happened to come to Maine, and to relate the experiences of our early years here, first on Daicey Mountain and a little later, at Baxter State Park. I believe that those days, learning the ways and customs of the North Country, meeting so many great, friendly people, and living close to the land made up some of the best years of my life.

Our early years in Maine never would have happened without the encouragement and the trust of my wife, Mary Jane. From the day we married, she entered into every decision to make a change, try something new, or travel a different road with a spirit of adventure. She was a good sport.

Everyone loved her, and so did I.

I dedicate the following saga to Mary Jane.

Foreword

During our seasons at Daicey Mt., I wrote many letters, a number of them to one couple in particular. In those letters I went into great detail describing our daily life and surroundings on the mountain. What a wonderful surprise it was many years later to receive a package in the mail containing all those letters which the Kings had saved.

Rereading my long-ago letters helped spark my memory in many ways, and the letters were a great aid in putting the first part of this narrative together. For that, I thank Dottie King for being so wise and so thoughtful.

In this book, I have mentioned some the nearby rangers I worked with and got to know well, but there were many more in the background. Although the group of us got together in the spring and fall, it wasn't until many of us, recruited by Hal Dyer, left Baxter and became part of the State Park System that we got to know each other better, and in some cases, become lifelong friends. Eddie Beach, Dalton Kirk, and Rodney Sargent have all enriched my life, and I thank them.

I also can't forget to give credit and thanks to all those friendly Maine people who accepted us into their lives so readily, so warmly, and with such graciousness. Most of them are now angels up in the Heavens over Maine, where I suspect they turn on those Northern Lights for me to enjoy.

Finally, and not in the least, I thank my present wife, who has put up with my preoccupation and moods each day as I've worked on this book. For her generosity, encouragement, and help in putting into writing a part of my life which she did not share, I thank Martha.

I love you too!

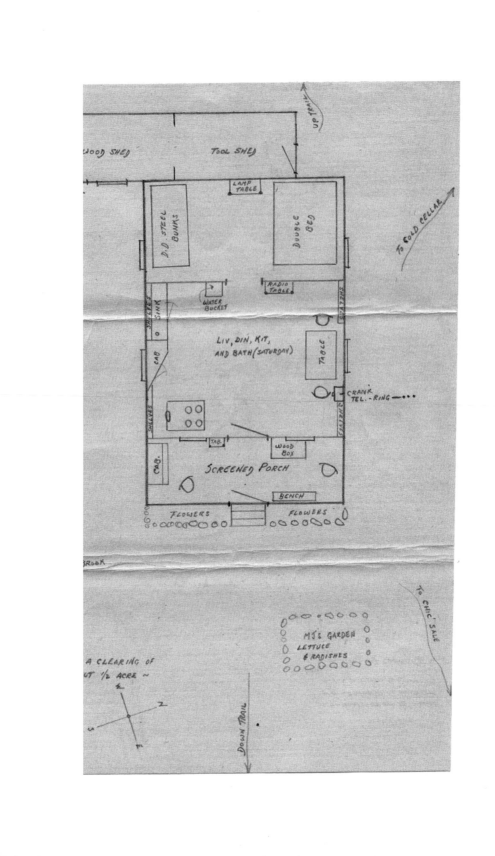

Contents

Ed at the Daicey Mt. Fire Tower

In the Beginning...

We, my wife Mary Jane, our two dogs, Pepper and Mickey, and I arrived in Stacyville, Maine, around noontime on a hot dry 4th of July, 1947, to report for my new job with the Maine Forest Service as fire tower watchman on Daicey Mt. Most of our worldly goods and our two not-exactly-tiny dogs had been squeezed into every corner of our ten-year-old car for the long, tiring drive from Connecticut. The final twenty miles, traveled over a dusty, gravel road through the deep woods from Medway, certainly was not the easiest part of the trip, but here we were.

Stacyville was a small town, a dozen or more houses, one of which held the post office. There was a small general store, and the Forest Service storage building for the East Branch District made up the rest of the town. It should be easy enough to find Prince Tracey, my new boss, I thought. No one seemed to be at the store-house so we drove a few hundred feet up the road to where Mr. Tracey's house and the general store stood side by side. Mary Jane suggested, "There are some men in the store, maybe he's in there." "I'll go see, you wait here."

It wasn't a very large building, but it was crowded with all the usual items of a small-town country store, except that toward the back was a pool table where my new boss, and another man were in the middle of a game of 8 ball. Now, Tracey probably looked up to acknowledge my presence, but if so, I didn't notice. Watching the game from a distance I began to get a little nervous at his seeming indifference to my arrival. Had he found someone else for the job? It had been several weeks since I wrote to him that I would take the position. Maybe I waited only a few minutes, but it seemed like an hour before that game was finished. Hanging up his cue, Tracey turned to me, "Hullo," he finally greeted me, "kinda warm, ain't it? Let's see if Nellie's got something cool to drink." Was I

1

relieved! Was this my introduction to the way of life and pace of living in upcountry Maine?

The three of us went to the house where Nellie, his wife, greeted us warmly, and soon we were snacking on lemonade, homemade cookies and donuts. After some small talk about our trip, the weather, etc., we got down to the business at hand. We could sleep that night in their trailer which was parked between the house and the store, then we would go upriver to our Mt. the next day, weather permitting. And, we could park our car and store some of our belongings in the Forest Service storage building, two details we'd been concerned about.

Most of the afternoon was spent sorting and planning what to move in to camp, keeping in mind that it would be a fifteen mile trip upriver with a half mile carry at Whetstone Falls, and then a two mile climb up the mountain to the camp. Prince told us that there probably were a few staples such as salt and pepper, flour, etc. at camp, but not likely much else. After we shopped at his store for what we thought we would need for the first week, we learned that the river patrolman would bring in further supplies every week to ten days depending on the weather.

We were definitely ready for some sleep shortly after a simple supper in the trailer, but there still were decisions to be made and planning ahead for the summer to be done. This was an exciting new experience for two "outsiders" and there were many questions in our minds which would not be answered until we were at the mountain, moved in, and on the job. Finally it was bedtime, but sleep didn't come easy

"What do you suppose the camp is like," wondered MJ.

"Probably quite small, maybe only one room," I replied.

"It's a long way from everything, what if one of us is sick?"

"So, we call Tracey on the phone, and he sends the patrolman in to bring us out." We thought about that for a while, and finally drifted off to sleep.

Maine Hospitality

Earlier that spring we had come to northern Maine for our third yearly camping and fishing vacation. Each trip had been planned by picking an area on the map that looked interesting — remote, unsettled, and fishy. This time we chose the Katahdin and Baxter Park country. In the back of my mind had been a dream that someday we might be able to own or operate a sporting camp in Maine. We had seen and visited some camps on previous trips, and developed a feeling that this would be a great way of life. It seemed to us the perfect way to make a living, and really enjoy being a part of the great wilderness country which we had come to love. Not that we were financially able to step right up and buy a set of camps, but I could dream and the Katahdin and the Baxter Park area sure looked good.

We camped and fished for a day or two on Millinocket Lake where, from our campsite, we had a wonderful view of Mt. Katahdin, Maine's highest mountain. Our map showed a road winding up into Baxter Park, ending near the base of the mountain, a road waiting to be explored. From Millinocket Lake we drove on toward the mountain on a paved road until we came to a turnoff onto a narrow gravel road. About a mile up that dirt road, the two Togue Ponds came into view, one on each side of the road. A set of camps and a Maine Forest Service station there were the only buildings we saw on that day trip. As we drove on, the next thing that caught my attention was a small clearing beside a rippling stream. I just had to try the fishing. Besides, it was time for a lunch break. It was a beautiful country and we seemed to have it all to ourselves, no other cars or signs of civilization. What a pleasant, peaceful place. Our map told us this was Rum Brook, but a cup of that icy cold water to wash down a sandwich was much better than rum.

"Listen, there's the sound of a white-throated sparrow," Mary Jane remarked. It was a song that had become associated with the

3

Maine woods for us, so we were especially pleased to hear it in that place. After lunch I cast a fly, not really caring if I caught anything as I was just enjoying being there.

Continuing on, the road through the deep woods became worse by the mile, but there were small ponds to see and the road crossed many little brooks, before coming to an end at another clearing by a larger, fast-running stream. A sight of the mountain from here presented an entirely different angle, now we seemed to be looking at the end of a sharp ridge. But, much as we wanted to linger, it was time to head back out, after what had been an interesting and enjoyable day.

The next day while making conversation with the proprietor of a small store near Millinocket, I asked a question, an off-hand query whose answer would start us on a path from one person and place to another, and bring us to a life-changing decision to move to Maine.

"Are there any sporting camps for sale in this area?" I asked.

"Not that I know of," the man behind the counter answered.

But, just before we left the store he added, "There's a fella has charge of camp permits for the Paper Company, they own most of the land and they lease some for camps. He may know of something." I got his name and address in Millinocket and soon we were knocking on the door of a neat little white house on one of the back streets. When I told Mr. Crommett the purpose of our call, and how I had gotten his name, he smiled and seemed to be somewhat amused, but he asked us in and introduced his wife Helen.

We spent a very enjoyable afternoon visiting with them, and Helen's homemade donuts along with a cup of tea were the best I'd ever encountered. We learned that part of Mr. Crommett's job with the Paper Company was to lay out lots, mostly on lakes, and issue permits to those who wanted to build personal camps. He knew of several commercial sporting camps in that part of the country, but none that were for sale or available at that time. Toward the end of our visit I voiced the opinion that it was difficult to get to know the country or find what we were looking for on short vacation trips.

4

Maybe if we lived up here we could make more and better contacts. He asked where we were headed from his house and I told him we'd seen a road on the map going north up through Stacyville and Sherman to Patten that looked interesting.

"Well," he suggested, "you might look up Prince Tracey in Stacyville. He's the Forestry Warden. There's a set of camps in on the river, Lunksoos Camps they call it, run by a young couple since the old man died. Prince would know if they figure to keep on there. And," he continued, "if you go in by Shin Pond from Patten, my brother has a farm, only one on the road past Shin Pond. You might stop in to see him."

When we left the Crommetts we felt we had made some new friends. They had lived in the woods and worked in camps and seemed sympathetic to our thoughts of wanting to make such a change in our way of life

That night in our tent on the shore of Millinocket Lake, we talked about what nice folks the Crommetts were and how much we had learned from them. We fell asleep listening to the drone of a mosquito in the tent and the call of a loon out on the lake.

It didn't take us long to break camp in the morning. We were anxious to get on the road to Stacyville and hoped to camp near Shin Pond that night. The road north from Medway more or less followed a river as far as Grindstone, a small settlement hardly large enough to have a name. There couldn't have been more than a half dozen camps and houses on the river. We stopped at a nice spot for an early lunch and, of course, to cast a fly in some fast water. It was a still, cloudy day, a good fishing day, but the black-flies seemed more vicious than usual so we didn't stay long. Looking at the road map I noted the river at this point angled away from the road in a northwesterly direction so unfortunately, we would not see it again.

Finally arriving in Stacyville, which wasn't a great deal larger than Grindstone, we had no problem locating the Forest Service building with its large sign out front and the typical brown paint on the outside. A man raking the lawn said Mr. Tracey was at his home not far beyond the Headquarters, and there we found him. After he heard how we had gotten his name and the purpose of our call we were invited in to meet his wife Nellie and talk some over donuts and coffee, donuts just as tasty as Mrs. Crommett's had been. When we inquired about the Lunksoos Camps we learned they were being run by a young couple named McMoran, and Tracy opined that they seemed to be doing all right, probably not thinking of selling. He, like Mr. Crommett, seemed amused with our ideas, but apparently took us seriously enough to suggest after a while that he had a fire tower position open on Daicey Mountain. "That would be a good job for a nice young couple like you for the summer," he said

It sounded interesting enough to want to know more about it. The lookout, he told us, was on a small, rather remote mountain reached by a fifteen mile canoe trip up the Penobscot East Branch from Grindstone. There was a nice little camp about two miles up the mountain and then it was another mile to the summit. Our food and supplies would be brought in weekly. The pay? About $170 per month. It was a seven-days-a-week job, but rainy days did not require my being in the tower, he added.

Well, this truly gave us something to think about, plus, we had enjoyed the hospitality of another friendly couple. The day was getting shorter, and we wanted to camp in the area of Shin Pond that night, so we said our goodbyes and headed north. Between Sherman and Patten we came onto a height of land with a spectacular view of Mt. Katahdin rising above the surrounding mountains like a sentinel. There was still snow on Katahdin, especially in the ravines. What gorgeous country! A hundred miles or more of mountain, lake, and stream wilderness stretched from there to the Canadian border and beyond. The Big Woods of Maine. The magnitude of what I was seeing held me spellbound until my practical wife reminded me, "We had better go, it's getting late to find a campsite."

We gassed up in Patten, since on the map, the road we planned to take west seemed to disappear somewhere in the woods. It did. It was rough and slow going. After about ten miles we crossed a bridge between Upper and Lower Shin Ponds and came to the Shin Pond House, a large inn standing on a hill overlooking the lower lake. The inn was also a store so we stopped to buy cigarettes and ask about a campsite. We were told there was a good Forest Service site about three or four miles further on, just off the road on Sebois Stream. It seemed the farther we traveled the worse the road became, more mudholes, ruts, and washouts. But, our rough ride was rewarded. The campsite looked great. There was a picnic table under a shelter and a safe fireplace right on the banks of the stream at a point where another small brook came in.

The sun had set and it was almost dark by the time our tent was set up, but sipping hot soup by a glowing campfire warmed our bodies and cheered our souls. The stream looked fishy, and my plan was to have trout caught for breakfast, so it wasn't long before we were snug in our tent beside a rippling stream in the woods of Maine. Just where I wanted to be.

The nights were quite cold that time of year and I wasn't surprised to find a skim of ice on the water pail in the morning. Wasting no time, I was soon casting flies on the pools and riffles of the stream, and had caught enough eight-to-ten inch brookies for a nice meal. MJ, bless her, had a good fire going by the time I returned to the camp site. It's hard to beat fresh-caught, native brook trout pan-fried over a campfire, and we left nothing but a few bones. Of course with the dawn had come hordes of blackflies, and while the Woodsman's Fly Dope helped some, those blackflies seemed to hover in a cloud around us, waiting for the dope to lose its potency so they could descend on any exposed skin. MJ's treatment for insect bites was a dab of wet baking-soda paste to ease the sting and itch, and it worked pretty well.

The rest of the morning we spent organizing our gear, gathering wood and just relaxing. On the way in from Shin Pond we had passed the Crommett farm, so remembering the Millinocket Crommett's suggestion, we decided to call on his brother in the afternoon. Again we found a friendly helpful couple, plus a place to buy fresh milk, eggs and butter at very reasonable prices. It seemed strange to find a farm so far into the woods, but we learned they supplied food for the logging crews and stabling for the crews' horse teams. When we brought up the subject of sporting camps, Frank Crommett told us about the Bowlin Pond camps. They were not for sale but Frank had heard that the owner, Wayne Chapman, was looking for help, and it just so happened that he was coming out the next day for supplies. It sounded like a good idea for us to meet him and at least talk with him. We were becoming more and more determined about moving north.

Mr. Chapman was a big rugged man about our age who listened more than he talked. He looked like a man who belonged in the woods. Our story was told again while we all had a snack with the Crommetts, coffee and would you believe it! homemade donuts. Chapman said, "I have to go in to Patten and I'll be going back into camp in the morning. Why don't you come in with me, see the camps, and stay over a night." I looked at MJ. She nodded and I said yes before we fully comprehended what we were undertaking.

The Bowlin Pond Camps, we were to discover, were about ten miles south of the auto road on the banks of the East Branch of the Penobscot river, some eight to ten miles upstream from Daicey Mt. Chapman said we could ride in with him on his buckboard which sounded fine. The weather had been cloudy and drizzling off and on for a few days, but the sun was bright with only a few puffy white clouds in the sky when we met Chapman at the end, or beginning, of his road. His team of horses was hitched to the buckboard, and he was loading boxes from a pickup truck.

"Good morning. You can ride or walk. Some folks would rather walk," was his greeting. The buckboard was a homemade rig using an old auto frame complete with wheels and tires, and modified to hitch a team of horses. The bed of the buckboard was made of planks and there was a simple seat up front. "Road's kinda rough," he added, "but, this rig works pretty good."

The seat would be a little crowded for three so I stood up behind MJ to start off. "Rough?" I thought of other adjectives to describe it. They call this a road?, I wondered. A road to us outsiders was a thoroughfare you drove an automobile on. A road in this north country could be just a trail through the woods that many years ago had been cut and cleared by men and horses to haul out lumber or tote in supplies. They are called hauling roads or tote roads accordingly, and most of those old unused highways have been taken over by bushes and trees, in some cases practically obliterated.

Well, Chapman's tote road was rough, two wheel ruts twisting, winding around natural obstacles, with trees and boulders crowding in on both sides. Mudholes, and rocks I did not think the wheels could go over. When the going got tough the horses strained a little harder at the driver's urging and on we went. MJ's knuckles were white, gripping the seat to hold on, but she gamely stuck it out. At the horses' first rest stop I jumped down to stretch, and decided to walk the rest of the way. I began to notice animal tracks in the road. They were so numerous that I called out to Chapman, "The deer and moose must use the road more than you do!" He nodded his head "yes." Sure enough, just before reaching the camps a beautiful doe leaped out of the road as we rounded a turn.

The camps set high on a bank overlooking the Penobscot River although it was much smaller here than alongside the Medway road where we'd seen it downstream. Several log sleeping camps in a row were more or less at right angles to the main camp. After introductions to Mrs. Chapman and their four or five year old daughter Carol, I helped unload the buckboard while Chapman took care of his horses. We talked and got acquainted over lunch, and then Chapman showed us around. It was just the kind of place I would have given my right arm to own and operate. Dreaming again.

We met a man named Ralph Dolley who was working there for the summer, and he sat with M.J. and me at supper. He said he liked working for Chapman, but he was not impressed with the wife's cooking. He had heard she'd been a Home Economics teacher, but he thought the meals in a sporting camp should be a little more hearty, satisfying. About that time his fork made a squeaking noise on his plate. " I must have stabbed a vitamin," he remarked dryly. Little did we suspect how Ralph would come to fit into, and affect, our future lives.

That evening enjoying the warmth of a crackling fire in the main camp's large stone fireplace, we talked some more with the Chapmans. They were indeed looking to hire some help for the fall hunting season ahead. "Chore boy" and "cabin girl" were the terms used for the positions he had in mind. Before saying our good-byes and leaving camp in the morning, we told Chapman we were very interested and would let him know as soon as we could. The way the pieces were beginning to fit together since I had asked the storekeeper about camps was unbelievable.

At Chapman's suggestion I had brought along my fly rod for the walk out. The road followed Bowlin Brook for a ways, and those deep, fishy looking pools surely held some trout. The blackflies and mosquitoes along the brook were the worst we had ever encountered, but the fishing was great. I could have caught more than we needed, but settled for just enough fat native brookies for a good meal. We had spent too much time fishing. It was still about eight miles to our car, and I knew we would have to push to get out before dark.

Continually brushing blackflies from our faces, and picking our way around the many mudholes by going into the alders and bushes didn't make for a really pleasant hike out. It wasn't long before we found it easier to slog through the water and mud. We were getting tired, and the weight of our packs increased with every mile. We did see game, several deer, and there were fresh moose tracks most of the way. It was dark, after nine o'clock before we got out, and MJ was bushed. A ten mile walk out of the woods had not sounded like too much, but it was more of a trek than we had ever attempted before.

Cold sandwiches washed down with several cups of hot tea, and we were ready for some sleep. This was before the time of the now-popular sleeping bags. Our sleeping gear was folding cots and blankets, and to keep the cold from coming up from the ground, MJ had come up with the idea of layers of newspaper on the cots under the bedding. It really helped. Thank god the blackflies went to sleep, or somewhere, at sundown. Just a few mosquitoes to contend with as we quickly dropped into deep sleep.

With the morning came the blackflies as usual, but they are just one of the things you put up with if you are determined to enjoy the woods. There were some sore muscles and tired feet too. No plans for hiking today! A breakfast of bacon, fresh eggs, and milk from the farm hit the spot, even though there seemed to be a slight seasoning of Woodsman fly dope! After the dishes were washed and camp was in order, it was time to head back to Connecticut. This North Country of Maine really had a hold on me. I was in love with it and its wonderful, friendly people. And I hoped MJ felt the same way.

Back Home

It seemed our vacation trip had turned into a quest, a search for a new and exciting way of life. I wasn't sure if MJ shared my enthusiasm and dreams 100%, but when we talked over all the angles, the possibilities, the gamble, she was with me all the way. Our minds were made up. Income would be much less, but so would our living expenses. How can you spend money when you are way back in the woods? Still, this choice would take us a long way from where we had both started.

Both MJ and I had grown up in Indianapolis, and we had both lost our mothers at an early age. While attending high school I lived with a family on the east side of the city where MJ was the girl next door, living with her elderly father and a housekeeper. We rode the streetcar to school together and before long we were doing our homework together too.

MJ's mother had sent her to dancing school when she was young, and as a teenager she still loved to dance. Many evenings at her house, instead of homework, we turned on the radio to listen to big band music and dance. MJ taught me to dance and to feel the music, and many nights her father had to remind me that it was time to go home.

As a youngster, I had gotten a taste of the outdoors as a Boy Scout, and later took advantage of any opportunity to go fishing or hunting. It was so good to get out of the city. The southern part of Indiana was quite hilly and wooded, which appealed to me and my family, so during the summer we took many Sunday afternoon drives to the country for picnics. While MJ taught me to dance, I talked to her about my love of the outdoors.

My father had remarried and, until a subsequent divorce, my sister Dorothy and I had a stepmother and a stepbrother. I lost track of that stepbrother, Marion, until we were grown when he, by then known as "Toot," became an important part of my life. After high school, I worked part-time at the same Packard dealership where my father worked, and on Saturday afternoons after the shop closed, the employees sometimes worked on their own cars. Dad was busy under the hood of his car when I approached him one Saturday afternoon and said weakly, "Uh, Dad, I'm getting married next Saturday...can you come to my wedding?"

A long silence, then, "Son, I'd like to, but I'm getting married that day, too." And we both did.

MJ and I married young and there's something to be said about starting out right in a relationship; our honeymoon had been spent hiking the woods trails in mid-winter at a state park in southern Indiana. A year later we moved to Darien, Connecticut to share a house with MJ's sister, Kate, and her husband Fred. I worked for Fred in his tree surgery business, but after about a year of working for a relative at something I did not adapt to very well, I went to work at Sears selling housewares. I soon moved up to selling plumbing and heating installations as an outside salesman on commission. Then along came WW II, and with supplies scarce, it was hard to make a living.

A friend working at Chance Vaught Aircraft in Fairfield suggested I apply and I worked there in tool purchasing for the duration of the war, after which I went to a position in their Experimental Test Laboratory. I had a good job, an office, a future, but I missed the outdoors which is why MJ and I headed north to Maine for yearly camping trips.

When MJ and I returned to Connecticut from that north woods vacation in 1947, we had been married thirteen years, had no children, MJ's father had died, and our families, even Kate and Fred, were all settled many miles away. We had no ties, no reason not to do what we wanted with our future. Every wedding anniversary had been celebrated with an outdoor experience. Hunting, fishing, and enjoying the outdoors had become my favorite hobbies, and MJ had learned to share and enjoy them. Since every vacation was a camping trip of a sort, our decision was obvious, easy.

The decision made, there was so much to do. Letters were written to Prince Tracey and the Chapmans accepting their job offers. We would spend the summer on Daicey Mt., then go to Chapman's Bowlin Camps in the fall. Giving notice to Chance Vaught Aircraft sealed the deal and, I'll admit, seemed terribly final. My position in an administrative job in the Experimental Test Laboratory was the best-paying job I had ever had, so I kept reminding myself: no more sitting at a desk, no more wearing a necktie, no more commuting 35 miles daily. A complete change. New horizons.

There were also practical considerations connected to a move as drastic as this one, or maybe I should say as drastic as this one seemed to our friends. Some furniture and personal things of course we wanted to hang on to, and arrangements were made to store them for the time being. Everything else we gave away or sold. Paring down our lives had difficult moments. MJ had to look away as our mahogany Governor Winthrop desk went out the door.

There wasn't much room in our auto trunk but I made sure to find a place for snowshoes, guns, fishing tackle and other outdoor gear, while a homemade roof rack held several well-filled cartons and boxes. MJ had insisted on a few choice items of her own including her ukulele and a battery-powered radio. Our old Plymouth coupe was loaded to the gills. Our prospective employers had not complained when we informed them we had two dogs, and we would not have made the move without them. They were "family," so into the car fellas, time to go!

Our first dog, Pepper, was a terrier cross who looked some like a miniature short-haired pointer. I had brought her home as a pup a few days after our marriage thirteen years earlier, so she was very much a part of our family. Mickey was our cocker spaniel who had run away from former owners and adopted us a year or so before. His tail had not been cropped so he looked sort of like a miniature Irish setter. They, too, seemed eager to head north.

During our twelve years in Connecticut we had made many very good friends, and goodbyes were not easy, but promises were made to get together when we were settled in Maine. Although our landlord and friends had been somewhat skeptical at first, all wished us good luck as our family of four headed north. Just maybe some were a bit jealous of our ability to take such a step, and our daring in actually doing so.

Upriver

But now, we were truly here in Maine, waking up to the day when we would begin the summer up on Daicey Mountain. Prince had shown me maps and charts in his office and explained the basics of fire spotting. His East Branch District had two lookouts, our Daicey Mt. tower just west of the river, and Lawler Hill tower east of Stacyville just beyond Salmon Stream in Benedicta. When one of the watchmen spotted smoke and gave Tracey a compass reading and an estimated distance, he could ask the other towers for a reading and plot a reasonably close location on a wall map by stretching strings along the compass lines. Where the strings crossed was the hot spot.

Most of the river patrolman's time was spent on the river checking fishermen's campfires from a camp at Whetstone Falls. Prince manned the office and patrolled the roads by truck, and Nellie answered the telephone and helped with office work. It was a fairly small district compared to some of the other forestry areas. I couldn't wait to get started, but that first morning was cloudy and rain threatened so the long-anticipated trip to our new home was postponed.

The following morning dawned fair and warm, and we were ready for the trip in to Daicey Mt., our home for the next several months. The plan was for me to walk in on a woods road with the dogs to the riverman's camp at Whetstone Falls where I would meet the patrolman, Mary Jane, and all our gear, or "wangan" as Prince called it. Wangan...one of the many new words or north country terms we would be learning.

We met our riverman at the store house. "This is Bink," Tracey offered. Bink was about as rough a looking character as I had ever been introduced to. Not really dirty, but shall we say, rather unkempt. His eyes were red and bloodshot, and my guess that he had been out on a binge for a few days turned out to be true. And

16

I'm trusting my wife into the hands of this character?

Everything was loaded in a pickup and off they went headed for Grindstone where the road and river met. Pepper, Mickey, and I headed west out of town on a pretty overgrown old tote road. Oh, yes, I was carrying an axe and a knapsack holding some lineman repair tools. I was following the simple bare wire hung on trees that would be our lifeline to the outside, ready to do repairs if need be. I had been instructed how to splice the telephone wire, replace a broken insulator, or remove blowdown where needed. Most of the

Bink, the Riverman, enroute to Daicey Mt.

insulators were within reach, but some were on trees that had grown and were not so convenient. Sometimes I would have to find a tree limb or something to lean against the first tree as a makeshift ladder to reach a broken insulator. It was six or seven miles in to the camp and I found enough work on the way to learn the knack of how-to. I needn't have worried about the dogs staying with me. Except for short sorties into the woods chasing a squirrel or just investigating a new smell, they were close by . It was an interesting morning, and I enjoyed the feeling of being alone and pushing into an immense area inhabited only by animals and birds. And I saw several deer along the way.

When I arrived at the Whetstone camp, Bink and MJ had been there long enough to have unloaded the canoe and gotten a lunch started. Their trip upriver had been uneventful even though MJ did say they bumped a few rocks. Bink seemed to be feeling some better by now, and we found that he had quite a sense of humor. It seems that before I arrived as they were preparing lunch, Bink had looked out the window and exclaimed, "Oh, my God, here comes my Indian squaw. If she finds me here with another woman, she'll scalp me." MJ was scared silly, but everything turned out fine. The "squaw's" husband came along too, and it turned out they were a nice couple from Stacyville who had been upriver fishing. We all had a good laugh over our shared lunch.

It was too late in the day to continue upriver, so after deciding that we would stay at the riverman's camp, Bink suggested we go fishing. We canoed upstream a ways to where a nice brook entered, Soldier Brook, Bink called it. It wasn't long before we had a good mess of trout for our supper. Needless to say after such a day, we turned in early after eating our fill of fried trout, canned vegetables and boiled tea. A short time after we blew out the lamp, MJ whispered, "I hear a mouse." I turned on our flashlight just in time to see a mouse run the length of the head-board of the bed. MJ ducked under the covers where she stayed until she was asleep.

As soon as breakfast was over we closed camp and started lugging our gear up the trail. The falls was a half mile stretch of very rocky rips and the Forest Service kept a second canoe at the upper end of the carry. Incidentally, the canoes were rugged 20' Old Town or White canoes, and it would have been a chore to lug one for that half mile stretch. Bink said the next stretch of water up to Daicey Mt. was quite smooth, so we could all make the trip in the one canoe. Three persons, two dogs, and 100 pounds of gear. It was a nice leisurely ride, but the 5 1/2 hp outboard had to struggle at times against the current. We saw two deer along the shore, and several flocks of ducks. Bink said they were mergansers that ran

18

along the surface before taking off. We were learning something new at every bend of the river!

Well, here we were at a landing near the foot of our mountain. We went around a point into a kind of back water or cove which Bink called Bark Camp Meadow. He told us that years ago this had been the site of a woods camp where hemlock logs were stripped before the bark was hauled to tanning factories down river, where the bark's tannin was crucial to the tanning process. But here now there was a small shack six or eight foot square with a tin sign on the door, "Prevent Forest Fires - MFS." This would be our storage building. The dogs were first out of the canoe, anxious to get on dry land, I guess. "There's a moose over there at the edge of the meadow," said Bink quietly. Sure enough we could see the dark shape of a moose feeding in the shallow waters. We just wanted to linger and watch, but it was time to get busy and get our "wangan" unloaded and push on up to camp. MJ loaded the backpack, then radio in one hand and ukulele in the other, announced that she was ready. I shouldered one of our large army duffel bags and Bink carried a box of supplies. Several cartons and boxes were left in the storage building to be packed up later. Two miles uphill to the camp. We stopped often to rest. The trail had been cleared quite wide and the telephone wire was strung along one side. The lower area was a mixed growth with quite a few large hemlock trees, but as we climbed, it gave way to mostly hardwoods. Finally we reached our camp in the middle of a small clearing.

A trickle of a stream ran down by on one side. On the other side of the clearing was our refrigerator. "That's your cold cellar," Bink explained. A sort of a cave had been dug into the side of the hill, then some walls, roof and a door had been added to make a small enclosure. In the coming months we found that it kept some foods quite well.

The camp of course had been shut up since the previous fall, so it smelled a little musty and stale. We got the shutters off and some windows open before taking a good look around. It was about 12' x 20' with a small screened-in porch on front, then the main room and last, the sleeping area which held a metal double bunk and a 3/4 size bed. In the kitchen was a small, four-lid wood cookstove, an iron sink set into a counter with overhead cabinets, a table and four chairs. Very basic. On the stove sat a greasy frying pan, and the sink held some dishes that needed washing. The floor could have used a good scrubbing, too. Bink explained that an old fellow had been there alone the previous summer. I half expected to hear MJ say, "I want to go home," but she pitched in and started cleaning house. I was reminded yet again just how lucky my choice of a wife!

Our Cabin on Daicey Mt.

"Can you build a fire?" Bink asked MJ. "There's wood in the shed," he added looking at me. The "old fellow" hadn't left much wood either, maybe a week's supply, so I knew what I would have to do soon!

"Guess we better have some biscuits," we heard as Bink pulled a breadboard out of the cupboard. He casually brushed some mouse droppings off with his hand and proceeded to pour flour into a sifter. His recipe seemed simple: he started with a sifter of flour, a lump of lard about the size of a goose egg, some salt, some cream of tartar, and too much soda. After working in the lard with his fingers, he added ice cold water from the spring to get a good rollable dough. He told us not to handle it any more than necessary. Cut out biscuits about one and a half inches thick, he said, and bake in a good hot oven. His biscuits that first meal were great and went well with our two cans of Dinty Moore beef stew. Bink's biscuit recipe was one we'd use many, many times.

The next thing I heard was, "Ed, let's get up to the tower." It was a mile of much steeper climbing and we were puffing some by the time we reached the top, even though we stopped to work on the line. What a view! Visibility seemed unlimited! There, due west, was that magnificent Mt. Katahdin, probably 12 -15 miles as the crow flies. In the valley below, the Wassataquoik River dashed southward over a very rocky bed to its junction with the Penobscot. There were rolling foothills and mountains in all directions, but to the east looking across the river a broad expanse of woods and farmland stretched to some hills across the border in New Brunswick, Canada.

The tower was not a "tower." The building, or cab I think it was called, was about six-foot square and was built on a base right on the rock ledges, securely cabled to all four corners. Glass windows on all sides of course. A round table about chest high in the center was covered by a map which mirrored the view and the skyline in every direction. Those magnificent views in each and every direction were certainly different from any in my last office!

"This is your alligator," said Bink adding, "It's a sighting device resting on top of the map similar to a peep sight on a gun." Bink went on, "You line up on a smoke and then read the compass bearing from the rim of the map. Then you look at landmarks and ridges on the line of sight to come up with an approximate distance." That was the extent of my instruction. I tried sighting in on a mountain or two and decided I understood how it worked. It was really quite a simple but effective system. Of course, I would learn later, the correct name was more like "allidator."

There was a chair in the tower, and of course, the state furnished a pair of binoculars. Bink put new batteries in the old crank phone and gave it a good long crank. Glory be! Nellie answered, and we were in business. After some further instruction on how to keep the phone in good repair we headed back to camp. Bink was in a bit of a hurry as he wanted to get back downriver to Whetstone before dark. We thanked him and said our goodbyes, realizing and appreciating what a good guy he was and how helpful he'd been in getting us started on our new job. Watching him head down the trail, I turned to MJ, "There goes our last contact with a person for a while." We were alone on our mountain.

At Home on Daicey Mt.

MJ had done some cleaning and straightening and the camp really looked livable. She turned on the radio and voila! there were stations all over the dial most of them speaking French as the Canadian stations came in loud and clear. It was getting dark so I found some kerosene in the woodshed and filled the lamps while MJ washed the chimneys. We were tired, but still had a few more chores to do. Make up the bed, wash up, and get ready to hit the hay. I guess Pepper and Mickey were ready too, as they'd each had found a spot to curl up under the bed after one last run outside. I'd like to say we both slept like a log, but that old mattress was lumpy and sagged in the middle. Adding some support under the mattress the next day, plus airing and punching it did help some.

It was a strange and exciting feeling...here we were all alone on a mountain in the big woods of Maine. The only person we would probably see the rest of the summer was Bink as we did not plan to go out until Tracey said it was time to close up camp. We'd actually done it, just as we dreamed! So much was new. Is that an owl or is it a fox barking? Sometimes they sound much the same.

Since the camp was on the east side of the mountain, it was good to see the early morning sun come streaming in the windows. I followed Tracey's instructions to call on the phone between 7:20 and 7:30 each morning for the day's routine. Nellie answered and passed on that first day's directions, "Prince wants you in the tower today, about 10 o'clock will be okay." She also informed me that our ring to answer was one long and three short. MJ packed a lunch for me. A goodbye kiss, and I was off with Mickey gleefully bouncing along ahead while Pepper preferred to stay home with MJ.

Another beautiful cloudless day. I took in the spectacular 360° view when I reached the top, and as I turned, my gaze stopped and was held again by the magnificence of Mt. Katahdin. I was looking into its glacial basins at what seemed to be about eye level.

23

Mt. Katahdin from the Daicey Mt. tower

What a sight. After opening the door and a window to air out the tower, I gave the phone a crank to confirm my arrival and of course Nellie and MJ both answered. Convenient, those woods phones.

A closer study of the surrounding country revealed some "smokes," but I was able to identify them as normal sights I would see most days. To the south were the stacks of Great Northern Paper's mills in Millinocket and East Millinocket. Southeasterly was a mill in Sherman Station, and way off in the east was some industrial smoke which the map told me was the town of Houlton. That circular map sure was a great help in locating places.

I called Tracey to verify my sightings then settled in to enjoy my first day on the job. He said he would send me in a new American flag to fly from the tower. It was convenient to have the cab built on the ledges with no superstructure as I could walk outside and still be conscientiously looking, which was the core of the job - looking, looking, looking for a sign that anything was not as it should be.

An old well-worn broom suggested that I sweep the floor and some cobwebs around the windows. A pile of magazines had to be moved uncovering a collection of old *Field and Stream*, *Fishing and Hunting*, and *Outdoors* issues. A most welcome surprise, they made for some interesting reading in days to come. During the morning my gaze kept returning to that mountain to the west. Through the binoculars I could see more clearly the detail of the barren ridges and peaks. As the sun moved toward the west the shadows and highlights were ever changing. That mountain was beckoning me, saying "Come climb me," and I knew some day I would.

I rang MJ while enjoying my lunch. She was still busy cleaning and arranging things for her convenience, and was already making a list of groceries and other items to order. Heading down the steep slope at the end of the first day, I continued to marvel at my new commute.

We were both settling in quickly, but there were still challenges. Mary Jane was finding it difficult to get a pail of water from

MJ lugging water

our small stream because the pools were so shallow. I found a small blown-down tree, dry but with a rotted-out heart, that I scooped out making a rough trough that I could set in the stream to give us "running water." MJ was tickled with this improvement.

Another challenge was the rapidly dwindling wood supply. Although fair weather required my attendance in the tower, I found that I could get in a hour or so in the morning and another in the evening of cutting trees and manufacturing stove wood. I was not a complete novice at this, but I did learn a few things. For instance, it was easier to get the wood into the shed if I cut the trees uphill from the camp, and I looked for trees, not too big, that grew straight and would be easier to split. The woodpile grew.

The outhouse stood on the edge of the clearing on the opposite side from the water supply, and MJ soon gave it a much needed scrubbing and deodorizing, as best you can a Chic Sale anyway. One day she discovered a spring not far, but far enough! beyond the outhouse in the woods. The spring water was cold, and a spot had been dug out by someone earlier to contain an additional cooler which we used to keep our milk and oleo, etc.

Our meals now were quite different from what we had been used to. If we ordered fresh meat it had to be used in the first day or two, so cured meats such as ham, shoulder, bacon, and salt pork became our staples. Back home we had often bought a smoked tongue which when cooked and sliced, good for sandwiches. We asked Prince to see if he could buy one to send in. One day we were advised the patrolman was at Whetstone with our supplies and would be in the next day. It was hot, dry weather and I was at the tower till late evening, so I waited till early the following morning to go down to our storehouse to pack up the supplies. Tracey had found a tongue for us, but it was fresh, not smoked. I don't know how long it had been unrefrigerated, but it was already crawling. We hung it up in the woods about 100 yards from camp for the bears, who had no trouble finding it!

Much of our food came in cans of course, but dried fruit such as apricots and prunes made a welcome change. Also we had brought a dozen or so jars of home canned vegetables which came in handy as were needed. Of course our milk was made from powdered products, slightly sweetened with a few drops of vanilla to make it more palatable. MJ jokingly called it "moose milk" one morning, and the name stuck. We tried to maintain as balanced a diet as we could under the circumstances. One of MJ's first cries for help to Nellie was for a recipe to make bread. Well, Nellie and MJ went back and forth, you take some yeast, dry that is, then sift your flour - how much flour? Well, depends on how many loaves you want to bake. It really came down to trial and error, but it wasn't long before MJ's bread was coming out beautifully.

Since it seemed that homemade donuts were standard procedure for the north country, and they tasted so great, that was MJ's next project, Nellie's recipe called for mashed potato in the mix. Delicious! Baking bread, donuts, cakes, cookies and pies and other cooking accounted for much of MJ's time, so we were soon ordering flour in 25# bags, and lard in four pound pails. Cooking also consumed a lot of stove wood so much of my spare time was spent on the woodpile.

But there was quiet time too. One hot evening we sat relaxing on the screened-in porch hoping to cool off some before we turned in. There was no breeze, no sound; a deeply quiet stillness seemed to surround us, when CRASH! We both jumped! "What was that?" MJ asked as we both calmed down a bit.

"It must have been a dead tree falling down," I guessed. It was. Big, old, dead stubs stand in the forest, and sooner or later they just get tired and fall. Many of course are blown down in windstorms, but that one I supposed just collapsed. Perhaps nothing stays still long.

Bink was a good guy, but apparently not very reliable. Tracey informed us he was looking for a new river patrolman. In the meantime an old-timer named Baptiste Rosignol who lived at Grindstone agreed to run our supplies upriver which he did the rest of the season. "Batiste" (his pronunciation) knew every rock in the river and hit quite a few of them regularly. He had a peculiar habit of ending almost every sentence with "of it." "I guess I hit a rock - of it." Or, "We need a new canoe - of it." After we became better acquainted I got him to smuggle a bottle of brandy in for us.

Batiste and Guests

One morning the inevitable happened. When I tried to phone Tracy there was no answer and no hum on the line. The trouble could be on the six miles of wire on my side of the river, or that ten miles from the river to town. I gathered my tools, axe, wire cutters, come-along, a splicing tool, and a coil of wire, kissed MJ goodbye and headed down the trail. All okay down to the river. From there downstream the line followed what I learned later was part of the old Telos Tote Road, a supply route used by tote teams during the logging boom. Another three miles and I came to Oren Brook where the wire disappeared into the woods, and I followed after it. I finally found the broken ends and dragged the wire out to the road. A moose had apparently gotten tangled in the wire. It was quite a struggle to bring the two ends somewhere near together so I could use the come-along which is a set of pulleys and rope with clamps to grip the wire. By this means you can hold the wire ends close enough to slip on a connector and crimp it. I got it done.

Well, time for a break, rest break that is. That brook had some nice pools so I had to try fishing it some day, I thought. There was still a mile or so of line to where it crossed the river so I figured I'd better check to make sure it was okay. No more breaks, but I did cut a few branches that were touching the wire. I soon came to the crossing where I could see the Lunksoos Camp on the other shore, but no sign of any people. All of a sudden there was a crashing in the woods off to my right where a large deer came charging out and ran right into the river. Close behind it came a fair-sized bear plunging into the water, too. The deer swam across unharmed, while the bear never noticed me as he turned and went back into the woods. It all happened so fast, I stood there hardly believing what I had witnessed. I hurried back to camp to tell MJ and have some lunch. When I called Tracey to check the line and tell him the story, he said, "Hmph" a couple of times, and then said, "Well, I guess you better go up to the roost for a look around." Just another day on the mountain.

On some nice days MJ would bring my lunch up to the tower and spend the afternoon. Although I never felt lonely on the mountain, it was good to have company sometimes. She enjoyed the views

MJ at the tower

too. There was a small pond down on the west side near Wassataquoik Stream, and often we saw a moose feeding there. Now, Daicey Mt. had two summits with a sort of saddle in between. I just had to see what that area was like, so while MJ was there to keep watch I explored. There were a number of mountain ash and striped maple trees down with most of the bark had been stripped off. I guessed that Moose probably had yarded there in winter, and someone later told me how the moose will walk a small tree down between their legs so they can eat the bark. I was learning new things about the big woods almost every day.

MJ came up to the tower one day and announced, "You need a haircut." She had brought a comb and the only scissors we had, a pair of manicure scissors. I sat outdoors on the folding chair and she snipped away for about an hour, while there was just enough breeze to blow the hair away. It sure wasn't anything like a barbershop cut, but it was a little shorter.

It was a hot dry summer our first season on Daicey Mt., but we did have frequent thunderstorms bringing welcome rain. They would come up in the afternoon and Tracey had told me I could leave the tower and go down to camp if I wanted. Well, after a few times of running down the trail beside a bare telephone wire in pouring rain with lightning all around, and sometimes fire dancing along the wire not too far from my head, I decided I would rather sit it out in the tower. It got pretty "hot" at times, but things sometimes got plenty hot down at the camp too. During one very heavy storm, MJ said a ball of fire came into the camp and almost knocked the telephone off the wall. (That time I had to replace the connector fuse (lightning arrestor) just outside the wall to get the phone working again.) So, I usually waited out the storms, especially considering that after any storm I would have to go back up again to check for lightning fires.

The tower cab, as it was called, was badly in need of a coat of paint, and the windows could have used some new glass and putty, so Tracey said he would send in some materials. I started scraping. The next trip in brought glass, putty, two quarts of white paint, and a 4" brush. It was kind of awkward using that large brush around the windows but I didn't complain. However, the paint was quite heavy so I did ask for some oil or thinner. Tracey sent me a bottle of motor oil. When I questioned mixing it in paint, he said, "That's what I always use, it'll do." Sometimes his ways were strange, but they did usually work.

A thank you letter to the Crommetts in Millinocket letting them know we were at Daicey had been the start of a close friendship, so it wasn't long before they decided to come in to see us. Tracey made arrangements for them to meet Batiste at Grindstone and come upriver with a load of groceries. They brought in some treats and we had a real good visit, mainly just talking and learning more about each other. Part of a day spent at the tower, I think convinced them that the view was hard to beat. It seemed to me that

Leon was still sort of amused with us and our dream, but he must have realized by now that we were dead serious. We had cut all our ties. We were here in Maine to stay.

My many hours of tower duty and long evenings at camp afforded plenty of time to write letters, so I wrote to friends and relatives to tell them about our new life on the Mt. Typical was the following:

"Arise about 6:30 A.M., build a fire in the cookstove and put on the coffee pot.

Helen and Leon Crommett

"Come on, MJ, time to get up.' Start cooking the bacon. Ring up Tracey at 7:00 to check telephone and get instructions for the day. The weather is fair so it's, "Well, it looks like another day in the roost, Ed.' Finally we have breakfast, eggs or hot cakes to go with the bacon. Toast is made on one of those old pyramid-shaped gadgets over the fire. Then it's carry water, fill the woodbox. Perishable food is put back in the cold cellar or spring. Lunch is packed, kiss MJ goodbye, and hit the trail."

MJ, too, often wrote to friends such as this note from July of 1948 :

"My day consists mostly it seems of cooking and baking. I thought I did a lot last year but so far this past two months I've used two 25# bags of flour and half of another. We have acquired the Maine habit of homemade donuts so that is another weekly duty. Along with baking bread, cookies, cakes and pies. Thank goodness I'm getting a lot of exercise, so not putting on too much weight. I wish I had a pedometer to measure the miles I walk carrying water from the brook, going back and forth to the cold cellar and spring with food, and of course to the outhouse. This is just in our clearing. Trips to the tower and down to the river every few days add a few miles too."

During WW II sugar had been scarce and we had learned to take our coffee and tea unsweetened. Now, with no cream available, we were learning to drink coffee black. "Moose milk" just didn't do anything for coffee! Also during wartime we had bought a cigarette roller which we still had and put to good use. It not only saved money, but the hand-rolled didn't taste as good so we smoked much less. Each evening we rolled a supply for the next day, just another chore on the daily list.

By the middle of the summer we had settled to a regular routine. MJ cooked and baked, kept the camp clean and in order and did a weekly wash, quite a chore in itself. Lug water to heat in pails and pans to fill the galvanized wash tub. Hand scrub the clothes using a well-worn scrub board. Lug more water to rinse, wring out by hand, and then hang out to dry. Sometimes she took the clothing to the little stream to rinse. It was hard to get all the soap out. Ironing was also a chore using one sad-iron heated on the woodstove. Beyond that, Saturday night was bath night. Lug more water to heat then try to squeeze into that same washtub to scrub yourself. Rinsing off the soap was done by having the other person pour cold water over you from a pail. We tried to give each other as much privacy as possible, but it was rather difficult at times.

After the bath ritual, we would try to find some good dance

music on the radio. At that time they were playing Eddie Arnold recordings which we enjoyed. If there were no good tunes playing on the radio, we made our own, MJ plunking her ukulele with me trying to follow along on the harmonica. It was our fun night, a relaxed time that even Pepper and Mickey enjoyed. One evening MJ and I made up own words to the song, "I Get the Blues When It Rains"...

We're never blue when it rains,
Stay home and chop wood when it rains,
No tower duty, no climbing up the trail,
Just keep the stove a-going and fill the water pail,
We never ask for the sun,
It just means we will be on the run,
The rain is a blessing,
It keeps Tracey guessing,
That's why we're not blue when it rains.

We could do pretty well for amateurs on a few numbers such as "Down in the Valley," "Peg 'O' My Heart," and "Red River Valley."

Batiste and guests

34

On the days our supplies came in the first thing we looked for was the mail, our one tie to the outside world. We wrote many letters to friends and relatives with the expectation of getting answers, and they didn't let us down. One couple in Connecticut who rated as best friends decided they just had to visit us and see where we lived. Charlie was one of my hunting and fishing buddies and MJ and Bertha were close as sisters. We arranged for them to meet Prince in Stacyville and come upriver with Batiste. It was so wonderful to see old friends, and what a great visit we had! Bert, as we called her, brought along her ukulele and their evenings with us were filled with music, not always good, but fun. Charlie did some fishing in the river and caught several nice bass. We all spent some happy hours at the tower enjoying the view and reminiscing. When the time came, it was kinda hard to say our goodbyes.

Daily Life on Daicey

A large doe deer showed up in the clearing one evening, so MJ started putting food scraps on a stump that was on the way to the outhouse. It wasn't long before she had the deer eating from her hand, then the doe brought her fawn, although the little fellow stayed at the edge of the woods most of the time. We took an awful lot of pictures with our old Brownie box camera. The buck with his antlers all in velvet came too, but not as regularly as the doe.

On the trails we often saw partridge, and if you looked quickly, sometimes you could see the little chicks scurrying for cover. Mama would fluff her neck feathers, spread her tail to a beautiful fan , then try to lead you away from her family. They could be very protective, and one time a hen flew right at MJ.

MJ feeding a deer

Blackflies were still very bothersome well into July, but not nearly as bad as they had been in the spring. We learned ways to protect ourselves from their bites, in addition to using Woodsman's

Fly Dope. Pant legs were tucked inside fairly heavy socks, and the cuffs of sleeves were snug. Sometimes even an elastic band would help. A bandana kerchief around the neck kept them from getting inside your shirt and we always wore hats. It might be a little uncomfortable in hot weather, but it was worth it. After working in the woods a few years, I guess I built up a kind of immunity to them as they didn't seem to bother me as much.

I knew it had to happen sooner or later, and I also knew it would be Mickey, the younger dog, who would tangle with a hedgehog. It happened while he and I were working on the line down to the river. Mickey usually stayed fairly close to me so when he dashed off I looked just in time to see him go under a blowdown and let out a yelp. He quickly came out with a face full of quills. Poor dog, it was his first experience with "porky" and he was crying and whimpering like a small child. I had my wire cutting pliers with me, so I sat right down and started pulling out quills. There were probably a dozen or more. It must have hurt awfully and I had difficulty holding him while I talked to him, trying to keep him calmed down. Finally I pulled the last one, and let him up. Believe it or not, he charged right back under the blowdown and got another mess of quills! After another session of pulling out those barbed arrows, I put a rope leash on him and headed for camp. I wondered if he would ever learn.

In addition to my fire tower duties, I read and reported a rain gauge measurement, and once a season I spread a sheet under a small spruce tree at the edge of our clearing and beat the branches to make insects fall on the sheet. These were gathered, put in containers and sent out to the Maine Forest Service as part of their program to control spruce budworm and other insects. There were other side jobs too. The trail from the camp down to the river was cleared and cut about twenty feet wide and I was to keep it mowed. The tools provided were a bush scythe and a bush axe which had a wide axe blade on one side for chopping and a curved hook on the end to cut heavy bushes. A scythe was not a tool I had much experience with, and in the hands of a novice can be a back-breaker.

I did use the scythe during the summer to help keep the grass and raspberry bushes from growing too high in our yard and when the weather was such that visibility was poor from the tower, but not raining hard, I worked on the trails. One section of trail down by the river was easy to maintain. It went through a stand of huge hemlock trees, and very little undergrowth. The needle-covered ground was soft and springy. Large trees always drew my interest and this area of tall straight hemlocks seemed almost cathedral-like. However, when September came Prince informed me that NOW was the time to get that entire trail mowed and cleared. He explained that bushes cut late in the summer would not sprout as heavily.

MJ on the trail

Early fall presented a different kind of challenge, too. It wasn't convenient to shop for birthday cards and gifts while in the woods, so when Mary Jane's birthday came in September, my best offering was a card made from birch bark. It became a tradition each year after that, and I think she must have liked them as she saved every one of them.

I always enjoyed outdoor work, no matter what I was doing. One day while mowing I heard a thump-thump-thump sound I had not heard before. The only thing I could identify it with would be an old one-cylinder engine off in the distance. It would stop, then start again. No, it couldn't be that, I thought. It was difficult to determine its direction or distance. Finally I walked into the woods where it seemed to come from. Up flew a partridge. He had been drumming on a log. I'd known that they did that, but had never heard one before.

Another new and unforgettable experience was meeting a bear face to face. We had had a three-day hard storm and were pretty much confined to camp. When the weather cleared it was a gorgeous day, clear and cool. We needed supplies from our shack down at the river, so after breakfast I shouldered the rucksack and headed down trail with Mickey at my side. I also carried my axe, the handiest tool you can have in the woods, and one I never went on the trails without. About halfway I heard a rustling off to my left and guessing it was probably a deer, I held Mickey by the collar and sort of sat back on my heels and waited. Pretty soon I saw black, and more black as a good-sized bear shuffled out into the trail below us. Mickey quivered all over, but I held him tight and he kept quiet. The bear had his nose to the ground sniffing as he moved, then when he reached the foot path he turned and came directly toward us. I couldn't believe it. Apparently the wind was right so he didn't get our scent. When he got to about ten feet from us I figured it was time to do something. I stood up and shouted, "Hey, you!" That bear was so surprised he spun around on the spot and practically flew down the trail and off into the woods. It was so comical that I couldn't keep from laughing. When I let go of Mickey, he took off after the bear but came back shortly with his tongue hanging out. Very exciting.

When I arrived at the storage building, there, in front of the door, was a mama porcupine, or hedgehog as they were known here, and her two little ones. Cute little fellows, but they grow up and they chew and, as both Mickey and I well knew, they have painful quills. After quickly putting Mickey on a rope, I shooed them off and checked the building and our cartons inside. There were holes around the base where an animal could get in. All okay for now, but this was one reason why we did not leave anything down there any longer than we had to.

Seeing wildlife had become quite a common event but it was always a thrill to observe the deer and the moose, to watch them in their own environment. Bark Camp Meadow with its shallow water, grasses and water plants was a favorite place for deer and moose, an area far enough away from roads and towns that very few hunters visited. Strangely though, I rarely saw any birds or small animals around the tower.

That first summer I spotted several small smokes along the river which apparently were fishing parties' campfires that were properly cared for and controlled. No problem. Then, one day at the tower I smelled smoke very strong, the unmistakable odor of a woods fire. When I called Tracey he said there was a fire over in the western part of the state. The strong winds had carried the smell many miles. It was a dry summer and there were a number of fires in other areas of the state. Another time when I had not been in the tower all day due to low clouds and poor visibility, I went out to get a pail of water after supper. The air was heavy of smoke and as I looked up I noticed there was actually fly ash coming down. I ran back into camp and told MJ I was going up to the tower, maybe there was a fire on the other side of our mountain. I grabbed a flashlight since it might be dark before I came down, and took off at a run. Probably set a record for a one mile dash up the mountain. When I reached the top and looked around, I was relieved to see nothing that looked like a fire, but the smoke was so thick it brought tears to my eyes. I called Tracey and he said there were a lot of large fires in Canada and a shift in the wind was probably bringing the smoke down to us. It was scary.

Days on the tower were never boring to me. I could look down on the nearby woods and ponds and the Penobscot River on one side, the wild swift-running Wassataquoik Stream on the other, and

I would imagine what it would be like to explore, to fish or hunt. I studied the distant hills and mountains, ever on the alert for the sight of a smoke. Most interesting to me was the view to the west where magnificent Mt. Katahdin dominated the skyline. What challenges it presented. What was beyond? When not admiring the ever-changing views, I found time to read those old magazines and even got drowsy sometimes when the wind moaned in the cracks of the window frames. It was such a soothing sound, and even the slightest breeze produced a low hum. I was at peace with the world and with myself. This, this is happiness, I often thought.

Moving Out

Our first summer on the mountain was coming to an end and our first winter in Maine was just ahead. When Tracey called and said it was time to move out, we started packing, carrying what we could down to the storehouse. The next morning Tracey called to say Batiste would be at Bark Camp Meadow about ten. After making sure there was nothing left out for the mice to chew, the last chore for me was to put the shutters on the windows. Finally it was "Goodbye camp, see you next year," and down to the river.

Batiste was a little late and as he came around the point and into our landing he said, "I guess I hit a rock, of it." There was water in the bottom of the canoe so we pulled it up on shore, turned it over, and stood looking at a hole the size of a half dollar in the stern section. Batiste guessed that we could fix the hole "of it" and he told MJ and me to get some spruce gum from nearby trees and chew it. I had heard that people chewed that stuff but had not tried it. Batiste showed us the best lumps to pick and we were soon chewing away. Not much like spearmint, but not too bad.

There were some roofing paper, cement, and nails in the storehouse and a tin sign on the building that read, "Prevent Forest Fires" in English and French. "I think we can fix that hole of it, " said Batiste again as he pried the sign off. As soon as the gum was pliable, Batiste plugged the hole, smeared some roof cement on the surface and cut a piece of roofing paper to cover the area, then he bent the tin sign to the shape of the bottom. While he held everything in place I drove the roofing nails with my axe. I wondered what Prince would think of our rough repairs but Batiste wasn't worried. "This old canoe is all done, need a new canoe of it," he assured me.

We loaded up, and as on our trip upriver, three people, two dogs and our "wangan" pretty well filled the canoe. Going downstream under outboard power is quite different from pushing upstream The motor is used to steer while you just keep going. The water was low after a dry summer and there were lots of rocks just under the surface. As we slid over several of them MJ, who was sitting in the middle on the bottom, would say, "Oops, we hit a rock." I would look at the patched hole and hope. The dogs lying quietly beside M.J. I guess just accepted this as another day in their new life in the woods. Some water did seep in, but the patch stayed on till we reached Whetstone anyway. There we carried our gear to the other canoe and continued on down to Grindstone where Tracey was waiting. He listened to our story about patching the canoe and agreed with Batiste that the old "White" had been on the river long enough.

We loaded the truck and drove to Stacyville where Nellie greeted us warmly.

The Traceys again let us stay in their trailer while we got ready to go to our next job at the Bowlin Pond Camps. Prince asked what our plans were for the winter. Our work with the Chapmans would be finished when hunting season ended November 30th, but there was a possibility of staying on through the winter just working for our board. Prince mentioned that the Beauliers just across the road had two camps in the orchard behind their house that they rented to hunters. We could probably rent one after the season. It sounded interesting so we went over to talk with Hal and Theo Beaulier. Hal was a potato farmer and was also active in town politics. They of course had heard about the city couple who were on Daicey Mt., and they seemed glad to meet us. After some conversation over tea and cookies we looked at the log cabins in their orchard. We could rent one for $10.00 a month and they would be glad to have us. The cabins were simple one room camps, but at least it would be home for the winter and according to Prince, I could probably earn some money cutting pulpwood. So we agreed to come back there after hunting season ended at Chapman's.

On that first night back in Stacyville, Prince allowed as how since we had been in the woods all summer we might like to go see a movie. "There's a movie house in East Millinocket and we can get an ice cream after," he suggested. I think it was the words "ice cream" that excited us the most. It was just what we needed, and we spent a very enjoyable evening with the Traceys. However, on the way home, somewhere on the Grindstone Road, we came upon a gory sight. A car had hit a moose and the game warden was dressing out the animal. He said the meat would go to a needy family. Fortunately, no one in the car was injured, but the vehicle wasn't going anywhere without a tow.

We also met Beulah and Stanley Sinclair at about that time. Beulah was the postmistress in Stacyville and was also Prince's niece. A room built on the front of their house served as the post office. Some years earlier Stan had been on the Daicey tower job for several seasons, so we had a lot to talk about. Stan worked in the woods in winter and he assured me I could find work too. Things were falling into place for the coming winter, a place to live and work to be found.

MJ and I had spent about four months together, mostly alone, in a life completely new to us deep in the woods of Maine. We had not had a spat and, as far as I knew, we had not gotten on each other's nerves. And we were already planning to come back the next year. My pay for that summer season came to $507.86 and our expenses were $149.32. That left us with $358.54. We felt rich!

Hunting Season

Before going in to Chapman's we needed some winter clothes so we made a trip to Island Falls to shop. Winter jackets, caps, mittens and boots were all purchased in one store, diminishing our new-found wealth somewhat. Island Falls wasn't a very large town, but we walked the streets so MJ could do some window shopping, then at supper time we found a restaurant where we enjoyed being waited on, and eating a meal cooked by someone else.

I also needed to pick up a hunting license before we went in to camp. While applying for the license at the town clerk's home, trying to convince her that we intended to become legal residents of Maine, we mentioned having been on Daicey Mt. all summer. "Oh, "she remarked, "I suppose you had plenty of deer meat to eat up there."

"Oh, no," piped up MJ, "I had a tame deer that I fed out of my hand, but we did have lots of partridge." I wanted to kick her, but instead changed the subject.

Everyone we met during that time in Stacyville was so friendly and helpful but much as we were enjoying their company, it was time to go. We telephoned Chapman and arranged to meet him at Shin Pond where we could leave our car. From there it was about ten miles in his truck to where his team of horses were tied. Getting there, we loaded our gear, a duffel bag and a knapsack, on the buckboard and off we went into the woods once again. MJ rode but I walked behind with the dogs and carried my rifle. Chapman said they had some bird hunters in camp but the deer hunters would not arrive until the first of November. We saw several deer and a moose on way in, the first of many more to come I suspected.

Mrs. Laura Chapman and their small daughter Carol greeted us warmly and showed us the cabin used by the help. I unloaded the buckboard while Wayne took care of the horses, and then MJ and I got settled in our cabin. Wayne and Laura both seemed happy to have someone to help with the work of which there was always plenty in a sporting camp. My main job as chore boy was to keep a supply of wood in the cabins and in the kitchen of the main camp and build fires in stoves when needed, work I'd done all summer. MJ as cabin girl would clean cabins and help in the kitchen and dining room, work she'd done all summer too, although both of us on a smaller scale. Of course we were also there to help with any other chore that needed doing. Chore boy and cabin girl, those were titles new to us, but as long as we were earning a living we could accept them.

Two of the camps at Chapman's

Bowlin Camps were in a nice location on the banks of the East Branch of the Penobscot River about eight miles upstream from our Daicey Mt. There were several log cabins in a row, the main building, and a hovel for the horses. Several ponds in the area could be reached by trails and Chapman's woods telephone line followed part of an old tote road known as the American Thread Road out to Patten. A company cutting birch for spools had used it in past years.

The camps had been built originally by Charlie McDonald in the late 1800's and were still in good condition. Across the river a trail led to an old out-camp on Messer Pond. Wayne said the pond was good fishing for small trout and some of his hunters liked that area. We went in to check on the camp which was at a fairly high elevation. That meant crossing the river by canoe using a setting pole instead of a paddle. It looked easy the way Wayne did it, but when I tried it the results were not the same. I needed to learn because when sports wished to cross Wayne wanted me to be able to ferry them. I never did really get the knack of it no matter how much I practiced.

One morning Wayne announced, "Today we're going to dip some honey." I wondered just what he meant by this, and I soon found out. There were a couple of of outhouses that needed cleaning out. They were built so the back side was open to reach with a shovel, so we dug a hole nearby then shoveled out the "honey" and buried it. One of those unpleasant tasks that has to be done.

The sports were beginning to show up so MJ and I were busy with our duties.

Mrs. Chapman did all the cooking while MJ set tables, peeled vegetables, did other chores in the kitchen, and of course washed dishes. Our meals were seldom the same as the guests. We often ate leftovers, and it seemed we had turnip most every day as the Chapman garden had produced a bumper crop of turnips. Much of the time during the day MJ was just babysitting the young daughter so Mrs. C. could do her work.

Our evenings were our own, and we enjoyed comparing notes about our day and reading by lamplight. The dogs behaved well, staying at camp, not bothering anyone. We had brought in a case of dog food and when that was gone we cooked muskrat carcasses and fed them the meat, which seemed acceptable to them. Wayne was trapping during November so we had a ready supply of dog food.

The weather turned very warm early that November and encouraged an unexpected hatch of blackflies. They weren't in a biting mood especially, but were real pesky, hovering around our faces. With the unseasonable weather, there were also reports on the radio of enormous fires in the southern part of the state. I wondered if Tracey might have had to send someone back up on Daicey. We did not learn the full extent of the fires until much later, and what we did learn was only by word of mouth. We seldom saw a newspaper. That was 1947, the year of the great forest fires, in Bar Harbor and York County especially. To us up there in the woods news of the fire didn't mean much. The amount of devastation elsewhere in the state just didn't really sink in as we'd had no fires in the northern area at all.

The camp telephone wasn't working well. It cranked hard and the voice was weak, indicating that the line was probably grounded. Wayne suggested I go out over the line to Patten where he would pick me up the next day. He arranged my overnight stay at a rooming house on the Patten end, and I set out. The line went close to Little Bowlin Pond and then southerly to join the old American Thread tote road and out to Happy Corner and Patten. There were many blowdowns on the wire and places where the insulators were pulled off the trees, giving me plenty of work to do. I was hanging the wire in one place where it was quite marshy, actually standing in water, when someone on the line cranked the phone to make a call, giving me a real good electrical shock.

It was late afternoon before I got out to Patten, a distance of about sixteen miles, tired and with no one had to rock me to sleep that night. In the morning there was a message that Wayne couldn't come in to pick me up. I had bought another case of dog food for our dogs, so I filled my knapsack with the cans and headed back over the line giving me a chance to double check for trouble on the wire. I arrived back at camp, even more tired, but with someone to rock me to sleep that night.

It wasn't all work. One day Wayne suggested, "Let's get some partridge for supper." I was all for it even though I hadn't brought in a shotgun. I was surprised when Wayne holstered a .22 pistol. We crossed the river by canoe and headed upstream on an old tote road that followed the river. Wayne mentioned that it was the Telos Tote

Road which had run from Millinocket up to Telos Lake. Those old tote roads had been used by teamsters to haul supplies in to the remote lumber camps, and now made nice hunting spots. It wasn't long before we were seeing partridge in the road. If they were close enough, Wayne shot them on the ground neatly clipping off their heads. Sometimes they would fly up into a tree and sit there waiting to be shot. Those birds had obviously grown up not having been bothered by the human race.

We were within sight of the river most of the time and passed by falls or pitches that were carries or portages for most canoeists. Wayne identified them by their local names, "Hulling Machine," "Grand Pitch," "Pond Pitch," and finally, "Haskell Pitch," where a huge rock stood upright in the stream. What a beautiful river. We had traveled about four miles, had plenty of partridge, so it was time to head back to camp with our birds. A very enjoyable day.

Another day Wayne said he wanted to check on a camp he had on Kimball

Pond about four miles by trail. He mentioned that it was also be a good chance to pick some cranberries. It was a good walking trail in to the pond where he also kept a canoe. We were soon picking cranberries from the canoe in a flooded area of the outlet stream. It was great picking, and we had a good mess to lug home.

The sports who came in for their week or two of hunting were all easy to get along with and were full of stories in the evenings about their day's experiences. One pair who hunted the trail up to Messer Pond across the river one day came back pretty excited. One of them had shot a bear. He said that he had met the bear head-on on the trail, the bear had charged him, so he shot the bear right between the eyes. Well, maybe so, but I had my doubts about the bear charge. It was a good season, and very few hunters left without their deer.

Thanksgiving had come and gone, there were no more sports, and we were beginning to plan our next move which was back to Stacyville. However, there was some new snow on the ground and I was anxious to do some hunting on my own before we left. The

49

rifle I had brought in with me although old was in very good condition, a nice Winchester carbine in 38.40 caliber. I started out early one morning with high hopes of bagging my first deer. The old tote road on the other side of the river seemed a good area to hunt so I crossed over and headed north. Before long I came upon what looked like fresh bear tracks going up-stream. I followed the tracks, winding through the trees for at least a mile, always hoping to catch sight of Mr. Bear. No luck. Soon I had to go around a blowdown of several trees, and while pushing branches aside, startled a deer who jumped up and took off from the other side of the blowdown. As he'd startled me too, I fired a quick shot, very likely without even aiming. A clean miss. There was no sign of blood or hair to indicate contact, but even so, I had tracked a bear and gotten off a shot at a deer on my first attempt at deer hunting, an exciting experience. Time to head back to camp.

It was also time to say goodbye to the Chapmans. We had learned some about the inner workings of a sporting camp, and the experience had not changed my hopes for a future in the business. However , the reality of the expense and effort it would require had begun to sink in. Our time at Bowlin Camps that fall had been an unusual experience for us of course, but I think it was the first time that my enthusiasm even wavered about the possibility of someday running our own camps. But heading into the winter, our pay for about six weeks of work came to $262.50 plus $40. in tips, minus miscellaneous expenses, leaving us with $287.00. Our bank account was growing.

Wayne called Elmer Wilson, a pilot who kept his plane at Shin Pond, and arranged for him to fly us out. The day we left was cold and windy as Wayne helped us carry our gear to Bowlin Pond to meet the plane. There was already enough ice on the pond for Elmer to land with skis, but it was so windy Wayne had to hold on to the wing while we loaded. It would take two trips so I went first with one dog, MJ and other dog following on the second trip. When we landed on Shin Pond the wind had swept the snow off leaving just plain glare ice and that wind just took hold of the plane and skidded us sideways across the ice. When we neared shore, Elmer jumped out and held the plane as best he could while I unloaded. It was bitter cold as I waited, and when MJ finally arrived too, Elmer suggested we go up to the Shin Pond House to get warm. It was a stiff climb up the hill, but certainly worth it. The Harveys, the Inn's owners, were very welcoming, and we soon warmed up with a snack of hot tea and cookies. Heading back out into the cold, blowy day, we found our old Plymouth waiting for us right where we'd left it. I had to get help to start the cold car, but finally we were loaded and on our way. .

Winter in Stacyville

When we reached Stacyville and the Beaulier's farm, we were treated to more of the generous friendliness we'd found so common in that country. Mrs. Beaulieu said there was no need for us to go into that cold cabin now, we could stay right there, warm with them. She had a nice spare room for us. The evening was spent visiting, getting acquainted, and answering questions about ourselves and our experiences of the past six months. Morning came and we moved to our newest home.

The cabin was made of logs, chinked with rope oakum, and it was set on posts. Just a single room with a sink and cupboards at one end, a wood cookstove, a table, two straight chairs and a rocker. There was one light bulb over the sink and glory be, a hand

Our winter camp in Stacyville

pump. We wouldn't have to carry water. At the other end of the room was the bed and chest of drawers. A linoleum rug covered part of the floor. Pretty simple, but MJ soon had it looking homey and comfortable.

There was some stove wood, but we would need much more to go the winter. I found that I could get a load of hardwood slabs from a nearby mill for six dollars. That was a start, but the cabin wouldn't be easy to keep warm as the west wind had a good sweep across the valley from Katahdin. Mr. B. gave me some bales of hay to bank around the cabin, and an old piece of canvas to partially close in the small porch. Even so, when the wind blew the linoleum would lift right off the floor and we were continually poking the oakum chinking back into the spaces between the wall logs. Sometimes snow would blow in through cracks around the windows too. I'd get up in the night to stoke the fire, but it was always out by morning. Didn't I shiver building a fire and waiting for that room to warm up!

It wasn't long before MJ with her outgoing personality got acquainted with our neighbors. They were families with children,

MJ, Mickey, and young friend

53

and as MJ loved children, our cabin became a place where the youngsters came to visit this new lady who read to them and told them stories. Sometimes there was candy or cookies for a treat. A few years earlier while living in Connecticut we had adopted a baby when we were unable to start a family. We had named him Charles, my middle name, but before the final papers were signed the mother changed her mind. It was a great disappointment to us, especially to MJ, and I understood her need to have children around. The neighbors' children were always welcome at our house.

Our first Christmas in Maine was quite different from those of previous years. I cut a small fir tree in the woods, made a stand out of scrap boards then stood the tree on a table by the window. We bought popcorn and cranberries which MJ strung on thread and draped over the tree. She cut out an angel from white paper and shapes of trees, balls, Santa Clauses and anything else that would look like Christmas. When these were hung on the tree it looked quite Christmas-y.

A few packages came in the mail from close relatives, but we were so busy getting ourselves ready, both physically and mentally, for the long winter ahead that we didn't take time out for shopping. Then, too, Millinocket, the nearest town to shop, was about a 70-mile round trip. Christmas Eve while listening to carols on the radio, we thought about the events of the past year. Our summer in the woods was really something to reflect on, a vacation with pay! Oh sure, it had involved some hard work, and maybe the novelty would wear off, but it had been a happy time full of new experiences and already we were looking forward to the next year. For the time being we had a roof over our heads, were in good health, probably had enough cash to get through the winter even if I didn't find work. And we had each other. These things, all of these things, were our very best Christmas presents.

The next morning when we went to the Beaulier's house for some fresh milk, Mrs. B suggested, "Why don't you folks come in for dinner? I'm cooking a big turkey and there's plenty for two more." The kitchen was full of the smells of the roasting bird, and pies were set out on the cupboards to cool. We were happy to accept the invitation, and MJ offered to help. When the Beaulier's daughter, her husband, and their five children arrived, the house just bulged with Christmas merriment, and we were made to feel like part of the family. Our first Christmas in Maine...what more could we ask.

Going to the post office was an important daily trip not only for getting our mail, but it also meant visiting with Beulah and Stanley. Before long, Stan told us that he and Beulah's father, Berdette Tracey, would be cutting pulp nearby in January, and I could join them. I would need a good axe, bucksaw, wedges, and a file and stone to keep the tools sharp for this new job. I found them all at the general store in Sherman, and soon it was time to start work in the woods. We were cutting pulpwood for a jobber who paid us $6 per cord, then he sold it to Great Northern Paper Co. Stan was a rugged, hardworking man, and piled his two cords regularly every day. Berdette, who was well into his 70's, had a steady, slow pace and averaged about a cord a day. I wasn't given the best cutting areas of course, and not being used to steady hard work, I did well to get a half to three quarters of a cord at first. I did improve some in time and we managed to pay our expenses as the winter wore on.

Some mornings when it was 20 or 30 below zero, we didn't get started any too early. It was always much warmer down in the woods though, and once we got working we could shed outer jackets. Keeping my bucksaw filed and set correctly and my axe sharp were important chores . Pulpwood in this case was spruce and fir trees, both heavy with pitch. The fragrance was quite pleasant, but our tools, which we cleaned with kerosene, mittens and clothing all got pretty gummy.

The best part of the day was the lunch fire. There was usually an abundant supply of dry cedar which made a quick hot fire to boil the tea. A stick propped at an angle to hold the tea pail over the fire was called a jill-poke, and when the tea boiled, the pail was set aside and a little snow tossed in to settle the leaves. When the weather was real cold, we warmed our frozen sandwiches at the edge of the fire. Along with eating, this was also a good time to sharpen your axe, and make conversation. I was learning many new words that were common in this north country, especially pertaining to the woods and lumbering.

Ed cutting pulpwood

A pole set upright with guy lines, and a rigging of rope and pulleys to move or load logs was also called a jill-poke. Logs were "yarded" to a clearing called a "landing," and your personal gear or gear accompanying a woods operation was your "wangan," a term I'd first heard from Tracey. There were also some new swear words which I didn't necessarily make use of. Berdette's included, "That jeasly tree fell the wrong way." or "There's a christly storm-a-comin." A person or thing might be called a "son of a whore," even though that wasn't used in a purely negative way. But that kind of talk was for the woods.

The Beauliers were good to us, and we were soon calling Mrs. Beaulier "Grammy Bo" as she was known to her daughters and grandchildren. In the fall she had saved a lot of drop apples from the orchard, and we could help ourselves to them and to the cull potatoes in the cellar. Also she churned butter once a week, and since MJ helped her some with housework and the churning we had skim milk to drink, and MJ learned to make cottage cheese.

Mary Jane feed us well that winter, not easy work for either of us. Keeping a supply of stove wood on hand was a continuous chore, but there were standing dead trees alongside the road and in the woods where we cut pulp, dead trees which I cut and hauled home in the trunk of the Plymouth. It sure took a lot of wood to feed that cookstove as it was a cold snowy winter.

Bink, our former river patrolman, was working for the Beauliers for his room and board, and one evening he stopped in at our cabin to visit. Before he left he told me there was a hindquarter of a deer hanging in a tree down by Swift Brook. He described where it was, but he did not say who had shot it! Taking my knapsack, flashlight, and axe, I set out and had no trouble finding it once I located his footprints in the snow. The cabin next door to ours was empty so I hung the meat in a back room. Our diet was helped a great deal that winter by deer meat, potatoes, applesauce, and cottage cheese.

A short time after I hung the deer meat in the other camp, a game warden called on us. We sat by the stove and talked for over an hour. He asked how we had liked our summer on Daicey Mt. and how we had happened to come to Maine. We had a good visit as MJ told him all about her pet deer, and how she had found the little fawn. Of course I was thinking of that hindquarter hanging not very far away from where we sat visiting. No mention of deer on his part, but all of a sudden he pulled out his service revolver and pointed it at the cupboard under the sink. "There's a varmint in there, want me to shoot it?" he asked. When I opened the cupboard door, a mouse scurried away. I guess it was his idea of a joke, but it sure startled us.

Our interest in operating a sporting camp got known around, and late that winter we heard of a camp for sale up near Patten. One nice day we decided to snowshoe the two or three miles from the road to the camp to see what it had to offer. We got directions from the owner, and were told the camp was not locked so we could inspect it. I guess his thinking was that an unlocked camp wouldn't be broken into, and there probably wasn't anything worth stealing anyway. On the drive to Patten we came again to that height of land with the exceptional view of Katahdin. Now, completely covered with snow, it was a breathtaking sight I didn't want to leave but with the assurance that we would see it again on our way back, we drove on. The camp was located on a small lake at the base of Chase Mt. I broke trail and took shorter strides to make it easier for M.J. with her short legs.

The camp turned out to be a rather old, two-story building with two fair-sized rooms on the ground floor which held a rusty wood stove, a heating stove and some old kitchen furniture. The second floor had four small rooms with old iron beds. Apparently it had not been used much recently, and the stoves were in pretty bad shape. Considerable cash, which we did not have, would be needed to make the necessary repairs, and buy the equipment needed to return that place to being on operating camp. Back to dreaming. Anyway, we had enjoyed the day, had tramped some new country, and had seen Katahdin in a different season's light.

Our Second Fire Season

1948. Spring finally came and the Traceys came home from their winter place in Florida. Ralph Dolley, the man we had met at Bowlin Camp had been at the tower on Lawler Hill in Benedicta, but now would become the new river patrolman. Because there was a lot of repair work to do, Prince put Ralph and me on the payroll early in April. My job cutting pulp had come to an end several weeks before, and I was anxious to get back to work.

On good days we worked on telephone lines, all told about 50 miles of line in the district. Some of it along roads was supported on poles, the rest in the woods strung, of course, on trees. One of the first things Ralph and I both had to learn was how to climb a pole wearing spurs and a safety belt. I had a tendency to drive the spurs in hard to make sure they wouldn't slip, but then it was difficult sometimes to pull them from the wood. After quite a few nervous climbs I sort of got the knack "of it," as Batiste would have said, but I did not look forward to days when we had to work on the pole line. Some of the poles were not set very deep and became loose in the ground when the frost went out, swaying and leaning when we climbed them.

"Put some shovels and bars in the truck, we have to go bury a dead man," Prince announced one morning. That didn't sound like a very pleasant day's work, so we were relieved when we found that the "dead man" was a three foot section of telephone pole. We buried it near a leaning pole, and attached a cable from it to the pole as a guy. Prince had gotten a chuckle out of our expressions and obvious relief when we learned the truth.

The woods line from Stacyville to Lawler Hill started across country from the Summit Farm and after about a mile went through what was left of an abandoned settlement called Davidson. There were a dozen or so empty houses in all stages of disrepair. From there, the line went by Davidson Pond and followed the outlet brook in a southeasterly direction across the Bangor and Aroostook railroad tracks and finally across Salmon Stream to the tower at Lawler Hill. From Tracey's house to Lawler Hill was about twelve miles, twelve fairly rough miles. Ralph and I spent several days working toward each other before we finally met and had a good line. Unlike our tower at Daicey, the Lawler Hill tower Ralph'd be manning was accessible by truck from Stacyville by way of Sherman Mills, Benedicta, and finally by driving through a farmer's dooryard.

When the weather wasn't good that spring, we cleaned and repaired tools and equipment. There were portable fire pumps to put in good running condition, canoes to patch and paint, and when there was nothing else to do we could always sweep the floor of the garage and shop. It was early in June before Prince decided to send me in to Daicey, Of course we had to move all our belongings out of the cabin at Beauliers, and store some things in the Forest Service building again, but it was nice to know we'd be back as we'd also made arrangements to rent the Beaulier's cabin again the following winter.

Ralph did a good job getting us up through the rips and rocks to Whetstone, and then let me drive from there on. He even offered to walk the telephone line from the crossing up to Bark Camp Meadow. I was learning the river, so I really enjoyed that part of the trip. After arriving at Daicey, Ralph stayed over one night and helped us get moved in. Ralph was an interesting fellow. He was sort of a self-taught naturalist, and apparently had read a great deal, so we found that we could learn much about nature and the woods from him. When he brought our supplies in he would often stay over a night, which made a pleasant break in our routine as we enjoyed his company. One of the things he showed us was where to find and pick "fiddlehead" fern shoots when they first came up in the spring. They grew in low areas along the river called logans that flooded during high water. Here we could pick fiddleheads by the bushel. Many folks came upriver to pick them, canning for the winter what they didn't eat fresh. Nellie told us how to cook them, and they were a tasty treat.

Working and living in the woods led to a desire to learn more about our surroundings, and it wasn't long before I could identify all of the mixed growth of trees in the area. When I found something new and different I could look it up in a tree book we had. I had worked for a tree surgery company in Connecticut for a year or more, so I had a good start. However, it was the many mountain flowers, plants and shrubs that Ralph helped us with. That became a fascinating hobby for both MJ and me, and being able to identify more and more plants brought us a great deal of pleasure and satisfaction. Our move to the Maine woods continued to be a learning experience.

Soon after we had settled in for our second season on Daicey, MJ's deer came looking for her handouts, but then those same cute deer became somewhat of a problem too. We wanted to try growing some vegetables in the old garden plot, so we had brought in some seeds and even a couple of tomato plants. Our clearing only got a few hours of sunshine each day, so our expectations were cautious. MJ put more cookies and scraps on the stump hoping that would keep the deer out of the garden. Didn't work! Although the deer and rabbits did get their share of the garden greens, we also enjoyed some fresh lettuce, green beans, beets, squash and cukes that summer.

Standing on the ledges outside the tower one afternoon I watched a couple of hawks soaring over the lower slopes of the mountain. I was actually looking down on them, and it was interesting to observe their hunting from my vantage point. My wonder was interrupted by the phone. I hurried back to the tower to hear MJ on the line, clearly upset. "I hear something crying in the woods. It sounds like an animal in trouble." She wanted me to come down right away to find out what it was. "Something is hurting," she kept saying. I couldn't leave the tower just then, but before we hung up, I tried to reassure her, telling her that maybe a fox had caught a rabbit. That did not satisfy her and she called me back to say she was going to investigate, and she wouldn't be talked out of it.

61

"Load the old .22 rifle and take it along, but don't go too far into the woods," I advised. The next thing I knew she was back on the phone, all out of breath and crying.

"It's a little fawn deer, and I carried it back to camp." She described puncture wounds on its back and neck so I told her to wash the wounds as best she could and pour peroxide on them. I'd be down as soon as I could get there. What a sight greeted me when I arrived. MJ had been baking when the cries came from the woods. Her arms and front were covered with flour and blood, and of course when she wiped away tears, her face took on a smearing of flour and blood too. The poor little fellow didn't appear to be more than a few days old, nicely spotted, but it was in bad shape. She had put it on the porch , and kept the curious dogs outside.

My best guess from the location and size of the punctures was that it might have been picked up by an eagle and then dropped. We had seen eagles over the river at times, and I knew that if a large animal had been responsible, it likely would have finished the job. We kept that baby deer warm in blankets and tried to give it some water, but in the morning it was dead. Nearby on the porch I found my rifle which I hadn't noticed the night before. It was also covered with flour and mud as MJ had used it as a cane while carrying the deer. It took me a while to clean it up and get the mud out of the barrel.

One morning Prince called to tell us that he and Nellie were coming upriver and planned to visit us at the camp. Mary Jane went into a tizzy, sweeping, dusting, and tidying up the camp. She always kept it neat and clean so there wasn't that much to do, but she did it anyway. Then she mixed up a batch of cookies to bake and put some fresh wildflowers in a glass on the table. Having company on Daicey Mountain was quite an occasion.

Mickey and Pepper reported them coming up the trail before we saw them. Prince was probably about 60 years old, tall and lean. He talked with a slow Maine drawl, and he never seemed to be in a hurry. A twinkle in his eye went along with a dry humor that came out at times. Nellie was almost as tall as her husband, but she looked somewhat younger than he. She was an outgoing, cheerful person and she and MJ got along great talking away about cooking, baking, knitting and such things. Their visit was kind of an inspection tour, and they seemed pleased with the way we maintained the buildings and trails and performed our job. And it really was "our" job as MJ was just as much a part of the arrangement as I was.

Prince, Nellie, and Ed at Daicey camp

That second summer was a good one, as we spent more time together at the tower, or "Roost" as Prince liked to call it. MJ would knit, or sometimes we played cards, casino being a good two-handed game. When I worked on the trails, MJ often packed a lunch and went along. She even tried cutting bushes with the bush-axe, but I discouraged that. We did not need any bad cuts from that mean tool. Working down along the river might include a stop at Oren Brook for a mess of trout, cooked and eaten right on the spot. What could be better?

I did manage to cut myself once, although not with the bush-axe. MJ wanted a large mixing spoon, so I decided to carve one for her. I got a piece of straight-grained wood from the woodpile and began my project while at the tower. It turned out to be quite a long operation, and one day the knife slipped and the point sliced into my forearm. It bled pretty good taking several band-aids to finally stop it. When I got down to camp later we washed the wound and poured peroxide on it. Then we made a butterfly bandage to pull the edges together and daubed it with carbolated vaseline, a salve supposed to have healing powers. It smarted some, but healed up real well.

Sometimes, due to the weather or other reasons, our supplies were delayed several days, and we would run short on some things such as eggs. Prince was always full of ideas on how to make do. "No eggs? Go down to the river where there's a gravel bar and dig some turtle eggs." We didn't try that one, but we did make tea by steeping yellow birch twigs in hot water when there was no coffee or tea. Prince had a good sense of humor, showing up in strange ways sometimes. Once he sent us in four cans of Dawson's Ale, which appeared on the grocery list as four quarts of oysters.

Beulah Sinclair, the postmistress back in Stacyville, sent word in one day that she and Stan had a friend from out of state who was going to fly up in his own plane for a visit. They would be flying over the area and wanted to know if there was anything they could drop off to us from the sky. It was the middle of July, hot weather day after day.

"Could you manage some ice cream?" we asked. Sure enough, when the day came, MJ and I were at the tower waiting for the "delivery." On the first run their plane buzzed the mountain and they and yelled 'hellos.' The next run was a little higher, and down floated two little homemade parachutes with containers of vanilla ice cream packed in ice. We had to search some to find them in the bushes, but, oh, didn't that taste good.

I never grew tired of studying the surrounding country. Every mountain, hill, valley and body of water held me in its spell of mystery, Katahdin most of all. What was on the other side of Mt. Katahdin? I wished I could see beyond. I looked down on Wassataquoik Stream hurrying southward to join the Penobscot, boiling over rocks and boulders, and its deep pools which, I just knew, must hold enormous trout. I could make out the lines of an old tote road that followed the stream up the Wassataquoik Valley to the Old City Lumber campsite, and sometimes I imagined the tote teams struggling up those rough trails with their heavy loads of supplies for the loggers. Sometimes, I imagined the families from Stacyville and Sherman who went in to pick the raspberries and blueberries that thrived after the Lumbering operation cleared the land somewhat. What stories and secrets these deep woods must hold, I mused many days.

I had had the good fortune one winter day when we were living in Stacyville to meet one of the men who helped open up that part of the country in the 1800's, and who knew some of the stories of the woods. Berdette Tracey, my woods co-worker, lived alone just around the corner from Prince on what was the beginning of the tote road in to Whetstone, and next door to Berdette lived Madison Tracey. "Mad," as Berdette introduced him to me, was well along in his 80's when I met him, and although his health was not too good, he did enjoy our visit. He talked some of his life in the woods. Mad told me that day that just below the site of the old "Mammouth Dam," near Old City clearing, there was a large boulder in the stream on which was chiseled "Tracey and Love commenced operations on the Wassataquoik October 16th 1883." He said that the lumber camps were moved upstream at a later date to what they called "New City" near Russell Pond. I'm sure he could tell many more interesting stories, and I hoped some day to actually see that boulder.

(I think it was his brother in-law who ran their lumbering business, but then there were so many Traceys that I was never sure of just how they were related . Sometimes I wondered why the town had not been named Traceyville.)

But as much as all of the area interested me, it was Katahdin, that huge mass due west of me that most frequently drew my attention. Its bare granite peaks and heavily wooded slopes were often hidden by low clouds, giving it an air of mystery. Were there people up there climbing its trails? What animals would one find roaming the woods? What plants grew there? It seemed different somehow from the surrounding country. I wondered how far up its slopes lumbering had crept. The basins on its east side facing me were, I learned later, carved out by a great glacier many years ago, and it had left ponds in the bottoms or floors of those gorges. Chimney Pond in the largest basin was on about the same elevation as the top of Daicey Mt., about 3,000 feet, so I could look right into it. The more I looked, the more I wanted to climb Katahdin's peaks and explore those basins.

Sometimes the moaning of the wind squeezing through the cracks and crevices of the tower would lull me to a half awake state, and images of long ago would appear: Indians who had hunted these woods, lumbermen, river drives. How different was it then, or did it really look very much the same from my mountain in the summer of 1948? I thought Katahdin might have some of the answers, and it was calling me...

Fall and Winter, 1948

We had had another summer with no major fires in our part of Maine, when, well into October, we awoke one morning to find two or three inches of snow on the ground. Prince phoned to warn us that we'd better get ready to move out. We already had done a lot of preparation, so we were able to close up camp and leave the next day. We had learned a lot about closing up camp for the winter. Any food left behind had to be in a mouse-proof container. The little devils would even chew the labels off cans and jars to make nests. Bedclothes and linens were hung up where possible and we would leave nothing that would freeze and break. Windows shuttered and doors secured. Winter can be hard on buildings in the woods.

We had not considered going back to Chapman's that fall, and then we heard that the camp had burned. Back in Stacyville, we settled into the Beauliers' cabin again and prepared for another winter which meant getting in the usual supply of firewood among other things. At least we now knew what the winters in Maine could be like, and we were prepared.

Through Ralph Dolley who lived in Sherman Mills, we had met quite a few new people, friends of Ralph's. One family, Sherwood and Ella Emery and their children, were very friendly and helpful, so when Sherwood invited me to go in to a hunting camp on Macwahoc Stream with him and two other men, I accepted quickly. It rained most of the time we were there, but although deer sign was plentiful, we shot no deer. Finally, hunting in a drizzle one day, I walked to within 30 feet of a small buck and shot it. My first deer! I was so excited that my heart was still pounding as I considered how to start dressing him out. I had dressed out many rabbits, squirrels, and birds, so I just followed the same rule of thumb or procedure, and managed to get the job done. Ironically, I was the only one of the party to get a deer, me the tenderfoot.

We hung the deer carcass in the empty camp next door to our home, cutting off steaks and roasts as needed. Our friend Berdette Tracey suggested we make some mincemeat with some of the less tender parts of the deer. He'd help us, he added. The first thing we needed for the mincemeat was some brandy. "It's no good without brandy," Berdette assured us, so we made a run to Millinocket to the "Green Front" as the state liquor store was called. We also bought some oranges and lemons, the only other ingredients we didn't have on hand.

Grammy Bo furnished a food grinder and plenty of apples so we were all set to go. Berdette came over on the appointed evening and settled into our rocking chair beside the wood stove. The first step according to Berdette was to taste the brandy to make sure it was okay. Then he sat and rocked as he gave directions. We ground the cooked meat, apples, nuts, and the oranges and lemons. "Rinds and all," directed Berdette. "That's what makes it good. Now put in the molasses and about a cupful of brandy, and it's about time we have another sip too," he added.

Berdette was dressed for cold weather, rubber shoe pacs, wool socks, wool pants, wool shirt and jacket. His usual ruddy complexion was getting redder than ever, but even though beads of sweat stood out on his forehead, he wouldn't shed his jacket. He just rocked and nodded approval of our labors. We sampled the mincemeat mix frequently now, adding more spice or more brandy to taste. When we decided the mincemeat was about right and had enough brandy, we finished off the bottle with a toast to...who else? "Mr. Brandy." When the mixture was finally put up in jars, we made sure Berdette had a good supply. It was darn good mincemeat!

The Traceys were going to Florida again for the winter and Owen Grant was still operating their little store, but apparently not to their satisfaction. Prince wondered if we would be interested in taking it over on a lease basis. It sounded good, but when an inventory was taken we found that we had nowhere near enough money to buy the stock, and with no collateral we couldn't go to a bank, so we gave up the idea of running the store. However we did make a deal with the Traceys to feed and look after their chickens in exchange for the eggs some of which we could sell to the store and some we'd keep for our own use. I think when spring arrived we'd just about broken even.

As the winter deepened, I started cutting pulp with Stanley and Berdette, but after the first week, Great Northern Paper Co. stopped buying wood from the jobber, so that was the end of that enterprise. Sherwood Emery had bought a large van-type truck and was hauling potatoes to Searsport where they were loaded on ships. He arranged for MJ and me both to work part time in a potato house bagging and loading. It didn't pay much but every little bit helped. Then Sherwood bought another smaller truck and set up a potato delivery route to grocery stores in and around Mechanic Falls in south central Maine. He offered me the job of driving the run which would be a two-day trip, and he even arranged to get a door key for a small empty store in Mechanic Falls where I could spend the night. Completely unfamiliar with that area of the state, I studied a road map to learn the locations of the towns and stores I'd be visiting.

It was mid-winter and temperatures were well below zero at night, so to keep the potatoes from freezing we installed a small wood stove at the rear of the van and cut a hole in the top for the smoke pipe. The truck was loaded with peck bags of potatoes and I hit the road early one morning for my first trip. The cab heater didn't work, and even though I wore all the clothes I could put on and still drive, it was cold! I expected to deliver potatoes at every stop but no — most of them had enough stock on hand. At the end of the day I headed for Mechanic Falls and the empty store with more than half the load still on the truck. By this time I was pretty discouraged, and felt as though I was coming down with a bad cold. The empty store was one small room about 12' by 20' with an iron cot for furnishings. All I wanted to do was get some sleep but first I had to build a fire in the stove in the back of the truck. The heat felt so good I sat by the stove for some time, but eventually it was

69

time to turn in. The old army surplus sleeping bag I had was cold but I crawled into it with most of my clothes on, and managed to get a few hours sleep. In the morning I phoned Sherwood for instructions and he said try to find more stores in the area if I could and then head home. It was another venture that just didn't work out.

About that time Leon Crommett got in touch with us regarding a camp that was available, and suggested that we, meaning our wives too, take a day to snowshoe in to Cedar Lake to have a look at it. Cedar Lake was several miles south of Millinocket, about three miles in from the nearest road. It was a fun day. The snow was deep and soft, and the gals kept tripping and falling. Then they had trouble getting up, partly because they were laughing so hard.

The main building of the camp we had gone to see had a large dining area and a good-sized kitchen. plus one room which could be used as living quarters. Two small log cabins stood on a rise nearby. Everything showed the effects of not have been inhabited for some time. When I asked Leon how much, he came back with "How much will you give for it?" Neither of us ever came up with a figure. I guess I was finally beginning to realize that getting into the sporting camp business was beyond our means, at least for now.

That winter, I worked with a small crew hand-loading four-foot pulpwood on a truck but soon found that I wasn't built for such a rugged job. From there I went to a crew loading logs for hauling to a sawmill. This was done by use of a jill-poke, the same contraption I spoke of earlier, a vertical guyed pole with a pulley at the top, and rigging of cables and pulleys attached to a tractor for power. A spreader of chain with a grabhook on each end was hooked on to the log and then the tractor lifted the log to a point where it could be laid on the truck. We rolled the logs into position with cant-dogs, pointed tools with a swiveled hook which grabbed on to the log. Pay was about a dollar per hour. That work lasted a few weeks.

One cold January night I awoke and saw a bright glare at the window facing the Tracy's house. I woke MJ and kept looked out.

"It's the store on fire," I realized as I started getting dressed. When I reached the store Owen was standing there in a daze. He probably had been sleeping in the store. As I asked if he had called the fire department and he said yes, we saw the red lights coming down the road from Sherman Station. The building was completely engulfed by then, the inside a boiling red and black mass of fire. The lone fire engine that arrived was a tank truck with a load of water that couldn't be pumped. It was about ten below zero and the pump lines had frozen. The firemen tried to get it thawed, but were helpless.

The Tracey's house was only about twenty feet from the store and the painted siding was blistering. Then we noticed some cedar shingles on the roof were smoldering too. Owen got a ladder and we took turns tearing shingles off by hand which was pretty hot on our backs and hard on our gloved hands, but we did save the house. The fire eventually burned itself out, and I went home to try to get some sleep. Apparently the fire started from a wood stove in the back of the store. That winter fire seemed almost ironic where I'd yet to see a real fire in my two seasons on a fire tower.

The long cold winter that year took its toll on all of us. Sometime in March, Mickey got lame and lost the use of his hind legs. We took him to a veterinary in Island Falls, but nothing could be done for him. He stopped eating and was quite helpless, so I had to make the decision to put him to sleep. We really couldn't afford to go to the vet again so I bought some chloroform and held soaked rags to his nose and mouth while I cried. It took longer than I thought, and I was a complete wreck by the time he was gone.

I found a place in the woods where I could dig a shallow hole and buried him. Of course anyone else in that country would have loaded the old 30-30 and shot him, but I just couldn't do it that way.

When Mickey had joined our family several years earlier, Pepper had sort of taken a back seat to the new, feisty, young dog. Pepper hadn't really live up to her name. Now that Mickey was not around, 14-year-old Pepper, who couldn't see too well and was quite deaf, really came to life. She wanted, and thoroughly enjoyed, some of the attention that had been missing for so long. A week after Mickey's death, Pepper was run over by a car that she didn't see and couldn't hear. Both our pets were gone. It was hard to take.

Spring, 1949

In addition to the Emery family, Ralph Dolley had also introduced us to Hal and Vee Dyer, a delightful couple about our age who lived in an apartment over Vee's parents' grocery store in Sherman Mills. Hal and Vee were so much fun to be with especially as MJ and Vee connected right from the start. We were beginning to enjoy more social life in the area, something which made the winter easier. We also met Archie and Marie McDonald who had a farm in Benedicta. It was Archie's brother Charlie who had built and owned the Bowlin Pond Camps before Chapman.

Hal Dyer had come home from war service, been appointed supervisor of Baxter Park, and then had convinced the Park Authority and the legislature to fund some development in the park. He planned to start building a campground at Roaring Brook which would be at the end of a road giving access to Chimney Pond and the Russell Pond trails, that same road we had explored on our first trip to Katahdin. During that summer when I looked toward Katahdin from the tower at Daicey, I pictured the crews at the foot of the mountain clearing the site for a new campground. I wondered if some day I might stop there on my way to climb Katahdin, which by now I was determined to do.

Ralph went to work for Dyer that spring, and Owen Grant was hired to be our river patrolman. Owen was becoming a good friend someone whose company we enjoyed very much. He came up for a few days to help me jack up the camp, to level and put new posts under the corners. There was no sense in lugging heavy screwjacks up the mountain so we cut a medium-sized spruce tree for a pry pole and with a couple of bodies hanging on one end managed to lift a corner of the camp. There are ways of doing things in the woods, you improvise. We got the job done.

While Owen was there we got to talking about MJ's and my future, and I mentioned that I'd been thinking about the possibility of building a small house somewhere. He said that empty houses in Davidson were being torn down to salvage the lumber, and I could probably buy some quite reasonably. MJ and I had managed to save up a few hundred dollars, so I decided to try to work something out. The possibility of our own house was exciting.

Late in the summer Hal Dyer offered me a job in Baxter Park, and I accepted. I would be a Park Ranger in charge of the Chimney Pond campground, the very spot in the great basin of Katahdin that I had been peering into for so long from my mountain. MJ and I were both excited with this new turn, and having said yes without even seeing the place, there was much to wonder about and learn.

Owen and MJ on the river

If I wanted to, I could start work in the fall when I finished the Forest Service job on Daicey, helping the crew at Roaring Brook until snow time. Now on those last summer days in the tower it was even more interesting to look over into that great basin of Katahdin, and to think what the future held for us in the park.

In the meantime Owen arranged for a purchase of timbers and boards for us for $200. Then, I made a deal with Ray Corliss, the owner of the Summit Farm in Stacyville, to buy four acres of woods on the edge of his farm for $50 an acre. Owen offered to help me build in the fall, but one thing held up the plans. Hal Dyer wanted me to start work as soon as we left the Forest Service. Dyer's crew was building the ranger's camp at Roaring Brook and he wanted to get it closed in before snows came, so we put off our house-building for a bit.

Things were happening fast. As much as we loved being on Daicey, this new job had more promise, and we would actually be living on Katahdin. After moving out from Daicey, we went right to Baxter Park where we stayed with the Dyers at the new headquarters building at Togue Pond while I worked with the crew at Roaring Brook. For so long Katahdin had called me, and now I had answered that call.

Of course we were anxious to see the cabin at Chimney Pond so, on the first available weekend, Vee Dyer, MJ and I climbed the trail from Roaring Brook to Chimney Pond. About halfway up the three plus mile trail we came to the Basin Ponds, a good spot to rest and enjoy the view. Looking out to the east we saw some small ponds and a larger body of water that Vee said was Katahdin Lake. A nearby mountain was actually two, the Turners, North and South, and looking past the shoulder of South Turner I could identify our Daicey Mt.

The trail became much steeper before we finally arrived at the Chimney Pond campground, a fairly level area in the floor of a large basin surrounded more or less on three sides by the almost-sheer walls of the mountain. The view was absolutely breathtaking. We were looking at an almost perpendicular rock wall rising over 2,000' with a jewel of a pond at its base. I was standing in the very spot I had admired from my Daicey Mt. lookout for so long. I had always known it had to be a beautiful place. As we stood on the shore of the small pond, Vee pointed out Pamola Peak on the left, with its knife-edge rim ending at Baxter Peak. From there a plateau sloped down to a low point at the head of the Saddle Trail which appeared to follow an old slide. Just to the left was the Cathedral

Trail, Vee added. It was so named because as it ascended there were several large rocky crags to climb over. It looked very steep. Turning more to the right a long ridge ran back to the east to a point ending in the area of Basin Pond. This completed the cirque surrounding the Great Basin.

The log cabin, our future quarters, sat back from the pond about 100 feet, and was typical, made of logs, one room with a sort of half partition separating the sleeping area, not much different from what we had become used to. I looked forward to living there. Several outhouses and log lean-to's were scattered around through the woods for campers. We ate a cold lunch at one of the lean-to's while Vee told us about a well-known guide named Roy Dudley who had lived at the camps. Dudley had made a living guiding climbers and hikers for many years until his death a few years previous, and he had a unique place in Katahdin lore. We would come to know his name well.

It was too late to try for a climb to Baxter Peak but I just had to try one of the trails while the gals rested. I chose the Cathedral Trail which wound through thick spruce and fir growth for a way, and then became steeper. I climbed until I could again look out to the east where the trail ahead looked to be almost vertical, a scramble over rocks and huge boulders. I took in the views in all directions. What a spectacular place to live and work! The sun had already gone down on the other side of the Mt. and the last rays touched some of the peaks. Time to go. Hurrying back to the lean-to, I found Vee and MJ anxious to start down the trail.

It seemed to me the gals should have been pretty well talked out by then, but there was a constant conversation going on as we descended. I tried to hurry them in the fading light, but the rocky trail made it difficult in places to find good footing and darkness overtook us about halfway down. Although I could see fairly well, the gals were having problems. I led the way slowly, carefully, but it seemed I was always waiting for them to catch up with me. At one point, while I was standing still, Vee spoke to me, and when I answered, she said, "Oh, are you over there? I guess I was talking

76

to a tree." That started them giggling. The little pocket penlight I had wasn't much help either, even as I tried to light the way when they needed it. Their talking and giggling never stopped, but at least, I thought, they're having a good time. However, it was a relief to all three of us to finally reach the Roaring Brook campground and our car for the ride to Togue Pond.

On another weekend, a party of climbers came in, and Hal sent me up to Chimney Pond to oversee their stay. They were a college outing club, a nice group of young people. I took advantage of the occasion to climb with them, finally reaching Baxter Peak and crossing the Knife Edge trail to Pamola Peak and back down the Dudley trail to Chimney Pond. The view from the top took in hundreds of square miles and there were lakes and ponds in every direction. Now I had seen the other side of the Mt. I had wondered about. It was a seemingly endless expanse of forests, mountains, and bodies of water, even more glorious than I had expected.

Late in November, work wound down on the mountain, and we headed back to Stacyville where Owen and I finally got started on the house. Building a house was a completely new experience for me, and I put my trust in Owen's knowledge. Mary Jane helped too, where she could. There were times when we had to build a fire to thaw the snow and ice off our materials, times of discouragement when something went wrong. However, by Christmas we had constructed a three room house set on stone and concrete posts, closed in and covered with tar paper on the outside. For heat and cooking MJ and I found a big old Atlantic Queen cookstove for $10, and a small steel airtight stove for additional heat. While building the house, I had kept Owen supplied with cigarettes and beer and he had taken most of his meals with us. Still, a bonus of $50 at the end was all he would take for his labors.

We were about ready to move in to our new home when we had a real piece of good luck. Sherwood Emery was hauling a load of Christmas trees to Connecticut so he offered to pick up our furniture which was still in storage there. We were excited at the idea of seeing our belongings again, and settling them into our own home

Our New House in Stacyville

One evening after we had moved in, but before the furniture came, Ralph Dolley arrived for a visit. Then the Dyers, the McDonalds, Vee's parents the Sleepers, and more of the folks from Sherman came. A surprise housewarming! They brought folding chairs, a card table, cakes and cookies. Ralph had even made a candy house with a padlocked door that when opened revealed over fifty one-dollar bills inside. What a wonderful surprise, and what a great feeling to be welcomed by these beautiful people.

Archie and Marie McDonald invited us to their New Year's Eve party, and of course most of the same folks were there. A delightful party, a great start to the coming year. Then when MJ and I went outside to start the car to go home, we could only stare in awe and wonder at the most spectacular display of Northern Lights we had ever seen. The entire sky was ablaze with flashing colors. Nature was really putting on a show, and it seemed, just for us. Happy New Year!

We settled in quickly, happy with our new home, enjoying the many friends we'd made, and knowing what a good decision we had made when we'd moved to Maine. And then, within the first few months in a "home of our own," MJ became pregnant. After sixteen years of married life we had about given up hope of raising a family. Was it because we had finally found real happiness? Maybe MJ's new friend Lizzie had the answer. Lizzy was a frequent visitor at the Beaulier farm where MJ had met her, and now Lizzy walked the several miles to come visit with us. She was a good soul and we enjoyed her company. Lizzie and her husband Lorenzo lived on the outskirts of town. "Renzo" was a woodcutter, making cedar railroad ties. They were good-hearted, simple people and lived simple lives, no automobile, no modern conveniences. They lived in a rough area, a town where family feuds broke out occasionally, a place where morals in some cases might not be too high.

Anyway, Lizzie arrived one day while I was out cutting wood.. As the gals sat rocking and gossiping, MJ excitedly told Lizzie that she had been to the doctor and learned she was pregnant. "Oh, my god, MJ, who done it?"

~~~~~~~~~~~~~~~~

The first winter in our new little house was mostly spent making it more liveable, no small challenge. I'd been using Owen's tools up until then, so I had to get some carpenter tools of my own, and the Sears catalogue was pulled out. I ordered a hammer, handsaw, level, and a tape measure, all for about $4.00, then set to building a small roofed entry way at the front door to protect against the wind and weather. After adding a woodshed on the back to keep our wood supply under cover, it was time to start on the inside. Ceiling tiles, window and door trim, and some painting all made house homey and comfortable.

MJ at our new house in Stacyville

We had no electricity and no well so we arranged to carry water in a 30-gallon milk can from the dairy farm. Thirty gallons is

79

a lot of water, and when the snows came, we hauled the can on a sled the half mile back to our house. With no insulation overhead, our roof produced the largest icicles we had ever seen, so I broke them off, melting the ice in a large kettle for extra wash water. Of course the two wood stoves ate up a lot of wood. Two of our four acres consisted mostly of hardwood trees so the supply was good, but burning green wood was not an ideal situation. Still, we were warm that first winter.

Although nearby Summit Farm had an unrestricted view of Mt. Katahdin, our little house was tucked into the woods where we were protected from the wintry winds. We missed seeing the mountain, but knew it was there waiting for us to return in the spring.

Perhaps this house wasn't much, but it was ours on our own land in Maine, the first property we had ever owned. What a great feeling! On top of that our family would increase to three in the Fall. Letters had gone out announcing the news to relatives and friends, and we began to wonder how this new development would change our lives. It was something to think about, as by now we had come to accept a life without a family. Everything seemed to be happening at once!

We become better acquainted with the couple who owned the dairy farm, and one day when I went up for water Ray said he could use some part time help. Pretty soon I was helping feed and clean up after the cows and doing other chores around the farm too, mostly shoveling — shoveling manure, shoveling silage, shoveling snow. It was a winter of heavy snows.

Our friend Lizzie continued to walk out from town to visit with Mary Jane, company that MJ enjoyed. One morning Lizzie came bearing a cake she had baked "just for Ed." It was a nice, big double-layer spice cake, a treat that looked very tasty. Fortunately Lizzie wasn't there at supper time when MJ and I had her cake for dessert. I cut good-sized slices for each of us, then took a bite about the same time MJ did. I looked at her, she looked at me, and we both almost choked with laughter. Apparently, we discovered later, Lizzie had run short of spices, and came up with the idea of using some of her husband Renzo's Old Spice shaving lotion. That cake was awful! We couldn't help laughing, but we knew Lizzie had meant well, and we appreciated the gift. I think Mary Jane told her later that it was not a good idea to use shaving lotion in cooking.

With MJ expecting, trips to the doctor became a regular part of our routine. The Dyers had recommended their doctor in Lincoln, which meant 100 mile round trips to see Dr. Mac, trips that gave us plenty of time to think and talk about how the new addition would affect our lives. Winters here in our little house in the woods would not be so much different with a baby, but 3000 ft. up on the side of Mt. Katahdin in the summer, well over three miles beyond the end of the road, and 26 miles from town...well, that might be a different story. I asked the mother-to-be, "Do you think we'd better try to make other plans?"

"No, we can manage, I think it will be wonderful, I'm not worried." There was no question about giving up that job as a Park Ranger at Chimney Pond. No sir. Once more, I was grateful to have a wife with such a willing spirit.

And so the days in our new home passed peacefully, until one night shortly after supper when we had a good scare. I heard a strange crackling noise above the ceiling. Looking up through the opening above the stove I saw the stove pipe was cherry red just below where it went through the roof jack. After quickly closing all the stove drafts, I climbed my makeshift ladder to see if there was anything near the pipe that could catch fire. The heat was intense, but there wasn't a thing I could do except wait for the chimney fire to burn itself out, and while it did, hope for the best. I assured Mary Jane that everything was all right and not to worry, even though I was still scared. That fire sure cleaned out the pipes and taught me a lesson: Take the pipes down once in a while and clean them the safe way as green wood causes a buildup of creosote in the chimney. And, that creosote is what catches fire.

We were too busy just existing that winter for much of a social life, but we did continue to visit with the Dyers in Sherman Mills, and got better acquainted with Vee's parents who had the grocery store where we shopped. Visits with the Beauliers who had rented us the cabin we had lived in during earlier winters were fun too. They taught us to play a card game called Pitch, and we enjoyed many an evening of cards topped off with a snack of Grammy's homemade pie or donuts.

Because Hal Beaulier was into Town politics and had been elected to the State Legislature, he was invited to go to the Governor's Ball, and he invited us too. Well, believe it or not, I still had the tuxedo that I had bought to wear when I took MJ to her sorority formal dance before we were married. The tux was packed away in a trunk and would have to be shaken out and pressed. Now, I really don't know why I'd kept it all those years, but here was an unexpected chance to wear it again, but what would MJ wear for the gala occasion? Her pregnancy wasn't noticeable yet, so Grammy Bo had the answer to that one. The Beauliers had a daughter who was about MJ's size and together they came up with a gown that was just right, one that didn't accentuate MJ's growing bulge. So with borrowed clothes and shoes, and after much preparation and primping, we were ready for the Ball and a night on the town. The Ball was held at the old Augusta House, a grand old hotel. It was a glamorous occasion and we were introduced to many dignitaries. MJ said she felt like Cinderella. The music was great and we danced almost every number. That was the first time we had had a chance to dance to an orchestra since leaving Connecticut, although we had kept in practice dancing to radio music in our mountain camp. It was a wonderful evening, and for a brief time we had stepped out of the woods, backwards in time, thanks to the Beauliers.

Work was hard to find that winter, but I was able to cut pulp for about a month on a lot near home. I didn't mind working alone, but did realize I had to be extra careful. Many a morning the thirteen-year-old Plymouth wouldn't start, so I'd get out the hand crank and try to turn it over, but temperatures of 25 to 30 below zero were just too much for the poor old car. So I walked the mile to my cutting. One day a partridge was hanging around my work area. It seemed quite tame, so when it flew up into a tree near me I was tempted. Picking up a chunk of wood, I threw it as hard as I could at the bird, and knocked it out of the tree. I really hadn't expected to hit it, but now I had to follow through and kill it. My next thought was why not cook it for my lunch. So I dressed it out, saving just the breast. As soon as my lunch fire was going good, I cut a small branch for a spit and propped it up over the fire. What a treat that would be to add to my cold lunch. Well, it was chewy and did not taste like any partridge I had eaten before. No surprise when I later found out it was a spruce partridge which were not known to be good eating.

Life on the Mountain

The spring of 1950 finally came and as soon as it was possible to get past the mudholes in the roads to the Park we, the crew, went in to Roaring Brook to work on the grounds and the new Ranger's camp. Because the camp was almost ready for the Ranger to move in, most of our time was spent burning brush and working on the future campsites. The crew consisted of Hal Dyer, the Park Superintendent, Fred Pitman, the Ranger at Katahdin Stream Campground, Ralph Robinson, who was to be at Roaring Brook, Ralph Dolley, newly hired for Russell Pond Campground, and me, newly hired for Chimney Pond. The "official" uniform for we park employees was pretty casual, dungarees and a flannel shirt, but we did have a badge to wear.

Even though the trails on the mountain were still choked with snow, I was anxious to get moved in to our new home for the summer. Hal Dyer and Ralph Robinson had purchased two burros the previous year to move supplies and equipment up to Chimney Pond, and now I was offered the opportunity to buy them. It would sure make hauling easier, saving us a lot of heavy backpacking of our food and gear the 3.2 miles up to camp. So for a little over $200.00 I bought Jack and Nancy, complete with pack saddles, bags, halters, and their stubborn personalities. Jack was a typical black burro, but Nancy was different. She was heavier, brown in color, and had a longer mane and tail, apparently a cross between a burro and a pony. As soon as the trail to Chimney Pond was clear I started learning how to handle the burros. Of course, first I needed to get acquainted with the critters, learn how to take care of them, how to put on their saddles and halters, how to pack the bags so the loads would balance. That was something, just one more thing in a growing list, that I had never dreamed of doing.

Jack had a tendency to kick when you were working around his rear end while Nancy liked to bite as many a camper later found out when they tried to pet her. Just getting those two donkeys started up

84

the trail was a lesson in patience and intrigue. With Jack's lead rope tied to Nancy's saddle, I would lead Nancy out of the campground. After a short distance I would turn them both loose and get behind them with a quickly cut switch to persuade them to keep going. That did not always work as many times that first summer they said "No," turned around, and ran back to Roaring Brook. That meant going back after them, retying their loads if needed and starting out again, probably going farther this time before turning them loose.

The trail up to Chimney Pond was a difficult climb for them,

MJ, Ed, and Jack

and I really couldn't blame them for their attitude. The upper part of the trail was quite steep and rocky, and sometimes it became a narrow gully washed out by rains and worn from travel. In those places, the saddle bags bumped against rocks and tree roots, which I'm sure bothered them. At one particular place there was a makeshift bridge, just three split logs laid side by side, spanning a gully. I noticed that Jack and Nancy walked only the center log, being quite sure-footed. Interestingly, I found that after we were about halfway up to camp, they did not have to be pushed so hard, there was no turning back as they knew rest and a feed of oats awaited them at the end of the trip. You might say that each trip was like completing an obstacle course, challenging to say the least. Jack had a carrying limit of about 100 pounds and if I tried to put more on him, he would just lie down, and refuse to get up. Not so dumb. Nancy, on the other hand, was quite rugged and could carry a heavier load, at times she managed almost 200 lbs.

On the right side of the trail, not far below camp was Dry Pond. Now that was a sort of a crater full of huge boulders, a hole which became a pond after heavy rains. Some grass grew around the edges, and there was a short trail cut through the thick tree growth, a path that had a pole barricade to close it off. That made a good place to keep the burros when they were not working. When I got to know more about Katahdin and the spirit of Pamola who reigns over the mountain, I learned that Dry Pond was Pamola's bathtub, and when he wanted a bath he used his powers to bring on a rainstorm to fill the pond. I almost came to believe that story because one day I might see the pond full of water after a storm, and the next day it would be empty.

We closed up the Stacyville house just before Memorial Day which was the beginning of the public use season for the Park, and started moving. I packed most of our clothes, bedding, and personal stuff and got it up to camp before MJ was ready to climb the trail. She was already about five months pregnant, but full of pep and just as anxious as I was to start our life at Chimney Pond. Sadly, this would be our first summer on a mountain without Pepper and Mickey.

Once again, there was a lot of cleaning to do in our new home. Mice had really had a good time in the cabin during the winter, chewing labels off canned foods and anything else that to them was chewable, and leaving plenty of droppings too. All the dishes and tableware had to be washed and the floors and tables scrubbed. Three years of living in one room camps on Daicey Mt. and in Stacyville, and here we were again. But this would be very different, for now we would also be talking to the public and registering park visitors in the one room where we ate and slept. And, the holiday weekend was coming up, when there would be our first campers and climbers to contend with.

By the time darkness closed in on our mountain and our new summer home on that first night, MJ and I were ready for some well-earned sleep, but first I had to go outside for a look around.

Our Chimney Pond camp

The massive walls of the cirque stood out against a star-filled sky. A soft breeze rustled through the trees, and the only other sound I heard was waterfalls cascading down from the ledges of Pamola. This must be pretty close to Heaven, I thought.

Stove wood was even more of a problem up here than it had been before. Cutting green trees was against the rules, so we had to depend on dead trees for firewood for heat and cooking. The Robinsons had used a two-burner Coleman stove for cooking during warm weather, and on the day Ralph was moving out he offered to sell their stove to me for $15.00. Money was tight, and when I hesitated, he suggested, "OK, how about we play a game of horseshoes for the stove." The shoes were old well-worn, and mismatched, real horseshoes. Two stakes driven into the ground among some rocks near the cabin served as pits, and if you didn't get your shoe into the gravely area around the stake, the shoe would bounce off a rock and fly into the bushes. It made for a challenging game, but somehow I won, and the stove did come in handy that summer.

Our water for drinking and other uses was carried from Chimney Pond which was less than 100' from the front of the cabin. Because of MJ's condition I carried the water most of the time, and when she did undertake that chore, I insisted on a half pail. That water was cold and crystal clear. Just outside the campground clearing on the downhill side, water came up out of the ledges to form a small pool which could be used by the campers for washing, which they appreciated.

As we had before, we settled in quickly, and it wasn't long before we were greeting campers and climbers daily. At times between packing trips when the burros might be tied to a tree near camp, they drew a look of surprise from climbers arriving from Roaring Brook who were not familiar with my packing business. One time Nancy was tied too close to MJ's clothesline holding a new wash, and MJ looked out to see Nancy chewing on one of my tee shirts. She also would eat pieces of cardboard cartons. Her eating habits were traits I thought only a goat would have.

In order to be able to give accurate information regarding the trails, I made a point of covering as much of, and as many of, the trails as I could when it was convenient. Each trail on Katahdin presented its own challenge, and each offered a different view of the surrounding country. My favorite was Cathedral, a steep trail making the hiker climb over 2000' in about a mile, at times using hands as well as feet for clambering over boulders and ledges. The climb, however strenuous, was well rewarded with views of the great basin to the left and right, views I never tired of admiring. Again, as at Daicey, I was getting paid for doing the kinds of things I loved most. What a life!

Many of our campers and climbers came poorly equipped and ill informed for the type of outing they were planning to experience. Some carried heavy backpacks or duffel bags weighted down with canned foods, heavy cooking utensils and other gear, some even carried glass jugs of water. On the other hand, some had no backpacks, carrying everything in their hands or hanging from their belt, with a rolled up blanket over a shoulder. Many of our visitors needed help and advice, especially if they were to stay safe on a mountain whose mood could change suddenly, quickly. It soon became obvious that an important part of our job meant looking after these people, helping them to enjoy their trip while keeping them out of trouble and harm's way, if possible. I say our job because MJ greeted and registered visitors when I was tending to chores around the campground, or on the trail. MJ was very outgoing, an extrovert if I ever saw one. She loved to talk with people, yet was just as good at listening No one really seemed to notice MJ's condition at first, or maybe they were just too polite to comment.

One of our greatest concerns for visitors was that the mountain seemed to make its own weather. Conditions could change momentarily, quickly becoming very uncomfortable, even dangerous, at the higher elevations. A hike that started on a hot, cloudless summer day might well end with cold rain and high winds. Improper clothing or shoes could very easily help to spoil a climber's day. Many times we loaned jackets, sweaters, knapsacks, flashlights, cooking utensils, and sometimes, we even shared our food. We considered it all part of our job.

Just as on Daicey, a doe deer showed up in the area, and it wasn't long before MJ was hand feeding her, naming her "Biscuits," since that seemed to be her favorite people food. Later in the summer a buck with a nice rack joined her, although MJ never did name the buck. Moose came wandering through the grounds once in a while to the delight of the campers, and the big animals were often seen on the trail too. Rabbits, also called snowshoe hares, were very numerous, and the birds at Chimney Pond were different from those we had observed at lower altitudes. Pine siskins chip-chip-chipped from the tree tops while white-winged crossbills and purple finches rummaged in the fireplace ashes. Of course Maine's chickadees were in abundance too. And then there was the gray jay, or "Gorbie" as they were known locally. They were so tame, seeming unafraid of anything. Hold a scrap of bread in your outstretched

MJ and Biscuits

hand and one would float silently down from the tree branches and take your offering, very unlike the raucous blue jay we were used to.

Wendell Tabor, a noted ornithologist, and his wife visited Chimney Pond that first summer, and he added a great deal to our bird knowledge. I believe he wrote a piece for Appalachia entitled "Birds of Katahdin." The Tabors were a delightful couple, and over the next few years they visited numerous times, and they joined our growing list of friends.

In contrast to our solitary life on Daicey Mt., we now were meeting new people almost every day, and enjoying the company of many. We particularly liked to welcome the young people, the Boy Scouts and also the Girl Scout groups who made regular trips to Chimney Pond from Camp Natarswi at Togue Pond. One day, a young GS counselor came to our door and rather apologetically said that her camp menu called for "shrimp wiggle," adding, "I don't know how to make the cream sauce base." After Mary Jane explained the how-to of cream sauce making, supper apparently worked out fine, but for the rest of the summer that counselor was known to us as "Cream Sauce."

One group of Explorer Scouts who visited was particularly enjoyable. Staff Rodgers, their leader, was an exceptionally good Scoutmaster in my estimation. He kept the boys busy doing different things, each a learning experience, and the boys enjoyed it. They cut extra firewood for us, carried water, and offered to help in any other way they could. One night, MJ made a cake in the largest pan she had and took it to their campfire where storytelling and singing went on longer than usual. During the evening a leader from another group came over, first to borrow a flashlight so he could find his flashlight. Next, he came back to borrow some matches. Then it was some sugar. Staff laughed, "Next thing he'll probably ask to borrow your toothbrush," but I think that fellow was angling for a piece of MJ's cake.

The view from our front porch at Chimney Pond was like something out of a picture book. It was just plain beautiful to me, almost overwhelming. Some might feel hemmed in by that towering rim of mountain almost surrounding the basin, but I never tired of studying the effects of changing light and shadows on the walls. When the weather was cloudy, rainy or cold, those bleak granite surfaces seemed to say, "Don't challenge me now, I'm in a bad mood." The emerging sun made all the difference in the world. The walls turned warm and inviting, and as the sun moved toward the west it created an ever-changing pattern, highlighting the surfaces and deepening the cracks and crevices. Then would come the rosy tint of the last rays of the sun on the tip top of Hamlin Ridge. A fitting climax for any day. I have no doubts that the changing moods of the mountain had their effect on me, and on anyone who spent much time in the Great Basin. For me it was almost spiritual.

Mary Jane was having no problems with her pregnancy, but the doctor wanted to see her on a regular basis for checkups, so at least once a month we went down to Roaring Brook, got into our old

Plymouth and drove the 40 miles to Lincoln and Dr. Mac. Back up the same day most of the time. MJ liked Dr. Mac, who encouraged her and told us that the exercise she was getting on the mountain was good for her. Of course the trips up and down the trail became slower and slower as the summer progressed and she became larger and larger. Some of the campers noticing her condition seemed quite astounded, and asked when she planned to move down off the mountain. Her answer was always, " I'll stay as long as I can, I love it here." Along about August someone gave us a small book, *How to Cope with a Home Birth*. I did study it some, particularly noting the advice on the last page, "However, if it's twins stick your head out the window and yell for help."

Aside from thinking about the possibility of our baby arriving at Chimney Pond or on one of trails, there were minor cuts, bruises and sprains among the visitors to contend with. Luckily, we had no serious accidents that summer. One day, however, a counselor from a nearby boys' camp group came to the door with a pained look on his face, and held out his hand for my inspection. Apparently he had fallen, bending the first joint of his little finger completely backward. This was something I had never encountered before, but I figured it was just a dislocation. I took hold of the end of that finger and pulled. It popped right back into place. His eyes bugged. "Gosh, it doesn't hurt any more. Thank you, thank you!" I realized all over again just how much a responsibility it was to be in charge of a campground so far from help.

Then one day, I too had a slight mishap. While pitching a game of horseshoes with a camper, a shoe bounced off a rock and struck me right on the knee. It hurt like blazes and was still hurting the next morning, so I decided to go out to Millinocket to have a doctor look at it, no light decision. I limped down the trail and drove to town. The doctor poked and prodded and bent the joint back and forth. "You came down from Chimney Pond today?" he asked.

"Yes," I answered.

"Well, then, I guess there's nothing much wrong with your knee," he said. "Just don't stand behind the stake anymore."

The days on the mountain went quickly. Most of the campers were wonderful people, and many evenings we joined families or other groups around a campfire for memorable times. MJ often made cookies and mixed Koolade for refreshments, and as we sang and told stories by the flickering light of those fires, we made some lasting friendships. As I mentioned earlier, we sometimes shared our food with campers who hadn't brought sufficient provisions of their own, and we were always glad to do that. Then too, departing campers quite often brought their extra food to us rather than carry it down the mountain. It was nice to receive a loaf of bread or a can of peaches, but we accumulated so many jars of mustard and cat-sup that we had to throw some away at times.

As the summer wore on, we began to hear more stories about Pamola who according to Indian legends, was the God of the Mountain reigning over the peaks and ridges of Katahdin. Pamola was described as part bird, part moose, and part man, certainly an interesting sounding combination. The Indians were afraid of him because hunters seeking the caribou had come to the mountain and never been seen again.

Prior to the 1940's Roy Dudley had been guiding parties from his base at Chimney Pond, and had been using the cabin where we were now living. Roy apparently was quite a storyteller, and claimed to have been on friendly terms with Pamola, even though it was said that Pamola did not like the idea of people climbing around on his mountain and disturbing him. Dudley's vivid imagination created a number of stories about his experiences with, and observations of, his friend, the mountain god Pamola. Telling those stories became Dudley's way of entertaining his guests on days when weather kept them from climbing.

I first heard some of the stories from people who had known Dudley, and after a while it wasn't difficult to picture Pamola sitting up on the Knife Edge, venting his anger while a furious thunderstorm sent daggers of lightning between the peaks. So when the weather turned bad and blew the roof off a lean-to, or brought a blanket of snow in late summer, of course we suspected it was the wrath of Pamola, unhappy with something we mortals had done to his mountain. I found myself retelling some of Roy's stories around campfires and more than half believing what I was saying.

(A wonderful book of Pamola stories is *Chimney Pond Tales —Yarns Told by Leroy Dudley*. Assembled by Clayton Hall and Jane Thomas with Elizabeth Harmon, and published by Pamola Press, it is still readily available.)

One of Roy's tales I liked and enjoyed telling was not about Pamola though. Of course, stories get altered in the retelling, but this is the way I heard it: On the wall of his log cabin Roy had a large assortment of fry pans hanging from nails. If someone asked where he got so many he would just casually refill and light up his pipe, and — Well, one summer he had a pet partridge that hung around camp. It came every day to be fed, and he became quite attached to it. When time came to close camp for the winter he wanted to be sure it was there the next summer, so Roy tied his largest fry pan to the bird's leg. In the spring when he arrived at Chimney Pond he was anxious to find out if the partridge was still there. He heard a lot of banging and clanging, and here came his pet with a whole family of little ones, each with a fry pan tied to its leg!

Here, as on Daicey Mt., we were dependent on an old crank phone for communication. Park Headquarters at Togue Pond was connected to the campgrounds at Katahdin Stream, Roaring Brook, and Chimney Pond, and HQ could call Millinocket almost 20 miles away too. The single bare phone wire was strung on small scrubby trees in many places along the Chimney Pond trail where moose frequently got tangled in the line, interrupting our service and requiring a quick repair job. At least by now, I knew what I was doing, and any needed repairs went quickly.

One eve as MJ and I were about to sit down to supper, a camper came in off the Mt. and told me he had talked with a man who planned to spend the night on the Plateau. That was very def-initely against Park rules, so I felt it was my duty to do something about it. Telling MJ to keep my supper warm, I took off at a run up the Saddle Trail figuring I could get up and back before dark, although I would have to hurry. The upper part of the trail was a steep gravelly slide which slowed me down some, but I soon reached the level area of the Plateau and located the young man. He was disappointed, but agreed to come down to Chimney Pond, especially as I really didn't give him much choice. I was hungry, in a hurry, and a little bit foolish running down the slide. My body got ahead of my feet, and I pitched headlong into a clump of bushes. Luckily I wasn't hurt other than a few scratches and bruises, but I slowed down the rest of the way. Supper, even that late and re-heated, sure did taste good.

Besides my regular daily work I was packing parties up from Roaring Brook quite frequently, enough to almost pay for the bur-ros. When Robinson phoned to tell me a party wanted to be packed it usually meant the next day, so I had time to plan ahead. I was still learning how best to get those two animals to cooperate .They were so unpredictable, I never knew what to expect. If I wasn't leading them, they might decide to go off into the woods anytime, or just stop and refuse to move.

It was a very busy summer for me, MJ, and the burros. Ralph Dolley who had been our river patrolman the previous year at Daicey was now the Ranger at Russell Pond, about eight and a half miles north of Roaring Brook Campground by trail. He made a point of visiting us whenever convenient and we again took advan-tage of his wide knowledge of the plants and flowers of the area. Among those we identified were the bluebells growing on the shore of the pond, and clintonia with its dainty yellow flower , growing right beside the cabin.

One day in June Ralph arrived at our camp on his way to Russell by way of the Northwest Basin trail. Since that was one trail I had not explored, I decided to go with him as far as Davis Pond, then he would then continue on down the north side of the mountain to Russell Pond. We climbed the Saddle trail which comes out onto the Tableland, a fairly flat area just north of Baxter Peak. We took time to look for some of the Alpine type flowers that bloom this time of year, flowers with names such as cinquefoil, saxifrage, twin flower and the sedges, if I remember rightly. The scrub growth of conifer that grew in clumps here and there were stunted due to the altitude, and although only shoulder high, they might be 75 to 100 years old. Ralph informed me that similar species growing in the high countries of Europe were known as "krumholtz," just the kind of interesting thing he'd know.

After a while we continued on toward the Northwest Basin, stopping once to look down into a wild-looking mass of huge boulders and scrub growth with a very small pond in the middle. It was a trackless area called the Klondike that would be almost impossible to explore. Eventually we came to a place where the plateau dropped off sharply. Looking down I could see Davis Pond, and to our left was another small pond with the unlikely, sounding name of Lake Cowles. I could throw a rock across it anywhere. Between the two ponds stood a shelter that had been built on the trail by the Appalachian Mountain Club. Because of its location at this high altitude, the shelter's only opening was so small you almost had to crawl into it. Not too far behind it, Ralph pointed out what served as a privy, a couple of 2x4s nailed together over a hole. Not very private, or comfortable to sit on. It struck me as odd that while Cowles seemed to have some plant life Davis had clear, lifeless water like Chimney Pond. My thinking was that since Cowles was the upper pond, and drained underground into Davis, maybe the rocks and gravel sort off sterilized the water on the way. I've seen that in several different places, the upper pond of two having life, while the lower pond of the two didn't. I'm still not sure why.

It was time for us to part company. Ralph had about five more miles to go to his camp at Russell Pond, while my trip back was almost that far. Before descending the Saddle trail I stopped to enjoy the view. The enormity of the Big Woods here in the heart of Maine was just so, well... BIG. About the only signs of civilization I could see were the stacks of the Millinocket paper mill some distance off to the south. I gazed over at Daicey remembering hours spent in the tower, and those many times when I inspected Mt. Katahdin through the binoculars. Now I am on top of you, Mr.

Mountain, I exalted! Chimney Pond by now was in deep shadows, and I had to hurry to make it down before dark. Except for Ralph, I had not seen another person on the mountain all that day.

Near the middle of the summer we learned that Hal Dyer was moving on to a new position as Commissioner of State Parks. I was certainly happy for him, but sorry that he would no longer be with us in Baxter Park. It was decided we would have a going away party for him at Roaring Brook and that a feed of brook trout would be a fitting dish for dinner. Robinson, the ranger at Roaring Brook, said he knew the best place to catch enough trout to feed eight or nine people, so on the day before the party he and I left Roaring Brook in late afternoon to hike in to Weed Pond. It was about ten miles into the heart of the Park, and we traveled light. Fly rods, sleeping bags, a small tarp and a light pack of food and cooking gear. Robinson led off at a fast pace, trying to show me up, I think, knowing I was not a native Mainer and not as much a woodsman as he was. To my secret delight, however, I kept up with no trouble. We followed the Russell Pond Trail until we came to Wassataquoik Stream. It was about 50' wide there, so we just took off our shoes and socks and waded into that almost hip deep, numbing cold water.

From there we followed the old Wassataquoik tote road downstream to a clearing I've mentioned before called Old City, the site of a bygone lumber camp. At that point we struck off into the woods toward a landmark Robinson pointed out to me, a pine tree that stood out above the others. That country had been lumbered and burned over the years and it wasn't hard going. We reached the pond in time to set up camp, eat a cold sandwich and try the fishing before dark. No luck. As darkness closed in the whippoorwills started their whistling song, which I had never heard before. Sleeping on hard ground was never one of my favorite pastimes, but the excitement of the occasion made it easier to take I guess, as I slept well until daylight when I heard Robinson breaking dead branches to start a fire. Breakfast was a shared can of beans warmed in a frying pan and tea boiled in a tin can. While we were

97

eating I heard a strange sound, ca-chunk, ca-chunk. Robinson said it was a bittern, a bird sometimes called a "sheit poke" or "pile driver." It was time to start fishing. Wow! The trout were hungry. They hit on any fly we tried. Ten-to-fifteen inch fish. Even though we put back any less than twelve inches, we soon we had all that we had come for. After the fish were cleaned we packed them in wet moss, broke camp, and headed for home. Needless to say the party was a success, and since Dyer was an expert at cooking trout he had the honor of showing us how.

Before Superintendent Hal Dyer left the Park he asked me to write my interpretation of the Chimney Pond Ranger's duties on a form for the Department of Personnel. What I wrote started with this paragraph:

"Operate the Chimney Pond Campground as a pleasant, clean recreational area for the public. Collect set fees for the use of the area, and keep accurate records of money. Be of service to the campers by giving freely of information and advice regarding the trails and surrounding country. Try to prevent accidents before they happen, but be able to give aid and assistance when required."

Of course there were other responsibilities such as maintenance, but those duties I believed were the most important.

The new Superintendent came on the job, but due to some personal problems he left the Park within a month, as did Ralph Robinson, the Ranger at Roaring Brook. Helon Taylor took over as superintendent and hired Myrle Scott as the new Ranger for Roaring Brook. It seemed like lots of changes in a short time, but it all worked out.

One midsummer day, Ralph Dolley was at Roaring Brook on his way in to his camp at Russell Pond with a good-sized pack of supplies. He'd been shopping and had a heavy load to carry in the eight and half miles. Ralph learned that a hiker had checked in at Roaring Brook and outlined his planned trip to Russell Pond by way of Chimney Pond and the Northwest Basin trail. I had talked with this hiker briefly when he stopped for a rest at Chimney Pond, then saw him on his way. By nightfall the man had not arrived at

Russell Pond, so Ralph, having no means of communication, no telephone or radio at the time, came out to Roaring Brook in the morning and phoned me to find out if the man had definitely left Chimney Pond. I assured Ralph that he had. Growing more concerned, Ralph came up to Chimney Pond and the two of us set out to follow the hiker's planned route up the Saddle, and over to Davis Pond in the NW Basin. At Davis, we could see no indication that he had stayed over, but continuing on we found footprints and signs that he had followed the trail, more or less toward Russell. That section of the trail, in a pretty remote area, was not very well marked. It followed the upper part of Wassataquoik Stream which it crossed and recrossed several times as it descended toward Russell Pond. By the time we reached Ralph's camp and had still found no sign of him, it was late in the day so we decided to spend the night.

In the morning we went back to the stream and located footprints which seemingly had to be his going on downstream. He had missed the fork in the trail which would have taken him to Russell Pond, and was now following the old tote road which ran alongside the stream to its junction with the East Branch of the Penobscot river, a long hike. As we continued our search down thru the Old City clearing, we came on blueberries, ripe and abundant, growing so thick I could reach down and grab handfuls without stopping. A welcome treat. After about four miles we reached Grand Falls, where we decided it made no sense for us to follow any farther, so we returned to Roaring Brook. The fellow eventually met a Forest Service river patrolman on the East Branch who helped him get a ride back to Roaring Brook, by way of Millinocket. We were glad to know that the hiker was okay, but it did strike me as rather odd that he had almost duplicated the well-known experience of Boy Scout Don Fendler, who had been lost on the mountain, some years earlier. We did receive a nice letter from our lost hiker, apologizing for putting us to all that trouble. All part of the job.

As the summer drew to an end visitors became less numerous, and after Labor Day scarce, except on weekends. The Saturday after Labor Day with the weather quite cold and rainy, a camper came in to visit and enjoy the warmth of our little cookstove, asking earnestly, "Gosh it's cold, do you think it's going to snow ?"

Mary Jane piped up, "Oh no, it doesn't snow this early up here," so naturally, there were several inches of snow on the ground the next morning.

By now MJ was very pregnant and everybody including campers began to be concerned about getting her off the mountain when it came time to have the baby. Then along came a couple from Houlton. When they arrived at Chimney Pond for the weekend it was very obvious the gal was also expecting, so it wasn't long before the girls were comparing notes. The "expected" dates were not far apart, and not very far away either. We enjoyed the Wetmores' company over the weekend. When they told me they planned a climb over Hamlin Ridge, I asked them to be on the lookout for mountain cranberries which I knew grew there and should be ripe for picking.

Now, mountain cranberries are delicious and I believe much tastier than bog cranberries. I had hoped for maybe, at most, a pint of the tiny berries, so when Ken and Louise came back from their hike and handed me a large bag of reddish-colored berries, I knew something was amiss. I tried not to laugh. It had been so nice of them to go to the trouble of picking them, but I just didn't know what we could do with several quarts of mountain ash berries. As the years passed and Ken and Louise continued to be regular visitors to the Park and the Mountain, we became better acquainted and in time, very best friends. And, too, our first-borns' birthdays were not very far apart.

But when we first met the the Wetmores, the four of us were still just looking forward to the births of our children. To be honest, I was beginning to worry some too about MJ being on the mountain, so about the first week in October we moved MJ down to Roaring Brook to stay with the Scotts until time for me also to move out. By now we were old hands at closing up a woods camp for the winter. There was no way to keep mice out of an old log cabin, so the only thing to do was get rid of any food not in cans or mouse-proof containers, keeping in mind that anything in a glass bottle or jar will freeze, break, and make a mess. One of the last things I did before leaving the camp at Chimney Pond, was to put about a dozen cans of beans, vegetables, and such in a burlap bag and sink it in the pond. It seemed like a good idea at the time, but come spring, we discovered that the labels had come off the cans so we had no idea of the contents, and since the pond had frozen solid so did the food. It didn't taste very good, but we did eat it.

The burros made their last packing trip moving our stuff down to Roaring Brook. We stayed on at Roaring Brook for a while with the Scotts, Myrle and Doris, and I helped Myrle build lean-to's in the new campground. Finally it was time to head back to our house in Stacyville. I had made arrangements to board Jack and Nancy at Summit Farm for the winter, but of course had to get them there first. Our old Plymouth had been traded for a more practical used pickup truck for which I made sideboards, but getting the burros loaded and moved to the farm was quite an operation, and one they were none too pleased about.

We had had some concerns about leaving our house all summer as it was in kind of an out-of-the-way location, but everything seemed to be OK when we got there. However, a mouse had been shut in, or had gotten in, and made herself to home. In the top drawer of a chest where MJ kept some of her best table linens, she found a nest of chewed cloth where a new family had been born. By that time MJ was getting used to putting up with mice, so she just decided, that, well, it could have been worse.

And Baby Makes Three

It was then late October, and another trip to Lincoln to see Dr. Mac brought the news, especially welcome to MJ I'm sure, "It won't be long now." And it wasn't.

About a week later, one night after supper MJ announced, " I think it's time we went to the hospital." She hurriedly packed a bag and off we went. On the way I kept asking her if she was all right. Her answer of "I guess so" wasn't very reassuring, but we finally made the 30-odd mile drive arriving at Workmans Hospital in Lincoln quite late that night. Dr. Mac was summoned. I spent some time with MJ, then went to a visitors room where, reading a magazine, I fell asleep. About six o'clock in the morning I was awakened with the wonderful news, "It's a boy," and both mother and baby were doing just fine. How strange it seemed that we were parents after sixteen years of married life, and what a blessing. Our son, Edward Gordon Werler, was born November 5, 1950. Our lives were about to change in ways both wondrous and unforeseen. Dr. Mac's bill for the delivery? $50!

Announcements of the new arrival had to be sent to relatives and friends far away, and gifts began to come in the mail. MJ's aunt Edith in Indianapolis sent a nice hand-knit sweater and bonnet that Eddie wore through several winters. Although I worked some at Summit Farm that winter, helping take care of #1 son took a lot of my time. The womenfolk had plenty of practical and welcome advice for Mary Jane on how to manage a newborn baby, and we felt very fortunate to have so many good friends, especially since we had been in that area only three years. The days and weeks passed, Eddie thrived, and the three of us settled into each other. It was a very special time in our lives.

But Eddie wasn't the only new life at our house as a creature took up residence in the woodshed for the winter. It seemed every time I opened the kitchen door to get wood for the stove a pair of beady eyes was staring at me from a pure white little body with a black-tipped tail, a weasel wearing its winter ermine coat. M.J. was a little fearful of it at first, but I assured her it meant no harm. and since weasels are meat eaters, I figured it was working on the mouse population. Always thinking of possible ways to earn money though, I momentarily considered trapping weasels for the pelts, but that idea didn't linger long. There must be better ways to earn a living.

Rabbits seemed to be plentiful in the woods, and rabbit stew made a good meal for a cold winter day. I was hunting on snow-shoes in a area covered with rabbit tracks one day, moving very slowly, looking all around, trying to spot a pure white animal, sitting still on the pure white snow, when all of a sudden a partridge exploded out of the snow at the tip of my snowshoe. My heart missed a beat or two before I realized what had happened. Even though I had heard that the birds would fly right down into the deep snow either for protection from the weather or from predators, that partridge sure gave me a start when it took off. I did bring home a rabbit that day, but those north country snowshoe hares didn't have a lot of meat on them, and what there was tended to be rather tough, so we learned it was best to make a creamy stew with vegetables added.

Sometime that winter, Ray Corliss, the owner of the farm, found a good buy on some maple-sugaring equipment and we struck a deal. For half the finished product, I would gather the sap, cut the wood, and help with the boiling down. We got started early in March when the days grew warmer while the nights still stayed good and cold. The farm had a nice growth of red maple trees where we worked together to drill the trees, drive in the spiles, and hang the gathering buckets. The buckets would then be emptied into the sap tank which I hauled with Ray's small crawler tractor. It was slow going because I had never driven a tractor before, and if I went too fast the sap would slop over the sides. On the first day I got the tractor hung up on a snow-covered tree stump. After that embarrassing experience I was more careful. When not gathering

103

the sap, I was busy cutting, splitting, and piling wood. It takes a l-o-t of fuel to boil down the sap, so luckily by that time I had hung up the old bucksaw and invested in a chainsaw. Sugaring was hard work, but the weather was nice and I enjoyed being in the woods. Of course I was new to the sugaring business, so I had to try drinking some sap. It was quite tasty, a little sweet, but not something you want to drink a lot of.

One Sunday M.J. brought Eddie and some children from town to the sugaring site to watch the operation and, they hoped, sample the finished product. They weren't disappointed.

Ray managed the boiling-down end of the operation, and under our deal, I think my share came out to be about four or five gallons of syrup which we put up in quart Mason jars. That's a lot of maple syrup, so I decided to try and sell what we couldn't use. Our friends bought some at $1.50 a quart, but we still had a surplus, so off I went to Millinocket where I pedaled it house to house. Even though Mary Jane had used syrup for sweetening in much of her cooking and we had eaten a lot of pancakes, we still had a good supply to take in to camp later. Although it didn't turn out to be very profitable, maple sugaring had been another new Maine woods experience for me, and one I had enjoyed.

Baby Edward had survived some digestive problems, which I guessed were not unusual for newborns, and we were all getting more sleep now. We were a happy family, the winter was almost over, and we were ready to move back to our mountain, and that season we'd be at Roaring Brook.

About the middle of April, I moved in to Roaring Brook where there was still plenty of work to finish the new campground, more picnic tables to build, a seemingly never-ending list. The burros were happily, I hoped, grazing with the cows at the farm, and I was not planning to bring them into the Park before late May, so they were not on my mind until a message came from MJ one day that one of them was sick. The events of the next few days went like this: Jack was down and would not or could not get up. A vet was called, and he thought Jack had a blockage. A sympathetic neighbor was trying to help MJ cope with the situation, and together those two gals managed to give the burro an enema. I'd like to have seen that! But, in spite of their best efforts, poor Jack died the next day. Several weeks later, for $75 I found another almost identical burro who became Jack #2.

About the first of May I started moving our belongings, and the family to Roaring Brook. This move was quite different from our previous ones. Now there was furniture, a bed, crib, tables, chairs, all that requiring several trips. It took a while to get settled.

Baby Edward was six months old, and now on the bottle so one of the amenities of the new camp, a gas refrigerator, was very welcome. The ground floor of our new home consisted of the small office in one corner, a kitchen, a bedroom and a living room. A staircase led to an open attic where we later put cots for company, while front and back porches completed the picture. In addition we had a large garage used mainly for a workshop and storage, a woodshed and of course, an outhouse. As the woodshed was on the way to the outhouse, we quickly learned to grab an armload of wood on our way back. With a baby to consider now, we very much appreciated this camp, so much larger and nicer than our previous camphomes, and of course MJ, yet again, soon had it feeling comfortable and homey. We would miss being on the mountainside up at Chimney Pond; we had come down the mountain but up in the world!

A sign outside the camp reading "Please register" was intended for parties who planned to camp at Roaring Brook; however, it also encouraged others to check in, whether they were arriving to picnic, hike to Chimney or Russell Pond or just walk over to Sandy Stream Pond to fish or look for moose. Our little office was often a busy place as we were giving out information and advice about a large area of the Park. Sandy Stream Pond in particular had become a popular place to visit because the fishing was good and the trout, although small, were plentiful.

When I wasn't in the office, there were plenty of other things to do. In addition to a considerable amount of work painting and finishing the interior of the camp, I built a desk and shelves for the office, and made a split-level Dutch door to keep people from walking into our kitchen. The open top also made it possible for MJ to keep an eye on the baby in the kitchen while she might be talking to people in the office. As always, MJ was working right alongside me, and our usual day averaged twelve to fifteen hours, but an unspoken part of our job was that we be available twenty-four hours a day. Eddie fit into our daily life smoothly, MJ and I shared a job and shared the care of our son, seamlessly it now appears to me.

Camp at Roaring Brook

Roaring Brook provided our drinking water, the nearest carry point being about 100' away from our cabin, upstream from the entire campground, at a bend in the stream where a Game Warden's cabin stood. Campers drew water anyplace from there to a spot downstream of the last campsite designated as the Wash Area. Since the Park had been developed, the wardens only used their building once in a while for family weekends, but I did happen to meet the warden one day while I was carrying water to camp. We had a nice visit, getting acquainted, and then just before we parted company, he stated, "You're going to have trouble with bears. They're a damn nuisance. Shoot the ba———-s." It tickled me to hear that from a game warden, but I soon found he was right.

The Russell Pond trail started with crossing Roaring Brook, either by hopping rocks or wading that cold, cold water. After about a quarter mile, the trail circled Sandy Stream Pond before heading north up the valley. Since Roaring Brook now had a Ranger and Sandy Stream Pond was becoming a popular spot to see moose, there was a need for a footbridge. Helon, who was settling into his first full season as superintendent at Baxter, came up to help me cut two spruce logs which we hewed flat on one side, then spiked together end to end, resting them on rocks. It served the purpose, but a strong rainstorm a few weeks later took our log bridge out as those mountain streams rose quickly after a storm. We put the footbridge back and it lasted until several seasons later when a real bridge was constructed.

On occasions MJ and I liked to take walks or short hikes with friends or campers., taking Eddie, of course. Carrying an eight-to-ten-month-old baby on the trail can be rather awkward , so I fashioned a suspended seat in one of our old baskets to hold him up for

Ed with Eddie in the packbasket

hikes to Chimney Pond and other places. It worked well, and Eddie seemed to like getting to know the Park and Katahdin from his high perch.

Mary Jane's sister Kate just had to see the new addition to our family, and a letter came announcing that she and husband Fred would arrive at the Millinocket airport planning to spend two weeks with us. It had been eight or nine years since we'd last seen them so it was a pleasurable reunion, with baby as the center of attention. Kate and Fred were childless and Kate got a great deal of pleasure from helping to bathe and care for the little one. Fred liked to fish, so he spent much of his time at Sandy Stream Pond. When time came for them to leave we were sorry to see them go.

That summer, too, we saw a share of visitors who should have come to experience the Park better prepared. Late one Saturday afternoon, two boys, maybe ten or twelve years old, came into the office, announcing that they planned to go to Chimney Pond that night, and climb the mountain the next day. Apparently a parent had just dropped them off planning to pick them up the next day, Sunday. Their inexperience was so obvious that at first it was funny, but it really was no laughing matter. "No," one answered when I asked if they had climbed before, "but my father has." They had one small knapsack containing several cans of beans, a loaf of bread and some utensils. Each had a blanket roll and a canteen of water hanging from his belt.. The rest of their gear, a jug of milk, a bag of potatoes, and an iron frying pan they planned to carry in their hands. I was astonished, and quite honestly, pretty annoyed with those parents.

Telling the boys it was a steep climb of over three miles to Chimney Pond, I suggested it might be best if they stayed at Roaring Brook for the night and go up in the morning. But, no, they were full of pep and raring to go. I could have insisted they stay, I guess, but instead, as soon as they were on the way I phoned the Ranger at Chimney Pond and warned him what to expect. Just about dark a couple coming down from Chimney stopped in at our cabin to check out. Had they seen two boys, I asked. "Oh, yes, they were sacked out at the first brook crossing about a half mile up the trail. We almost stepped on them," added the man. Well, as long as they didn't build a fire, I figured they were as well off there as anywhere. The boys did get to Chimney Pond the next morning, but apparently they went no further. Sunday was a busy day for me, and since they failed to stop in the office to check out, I missed seeing them again.

Visitors like that made us appreciate even more those who came well equipped. A Boy Scout group staying at Roaring Brook for one night before packing to Chimney Pond all had pack frames each had made as a project. The frames were wood, lightweight and padded in the right places. When I admired the frames and the fact the boys had made their own, the Scoutmaster promised to leave one for me when they left, which he did. It wasn't long before I was loaning that one and a couple more that I made, to parties not so well prepared for packing.

Using our two burros, I also frequently packed supplies or equipment to Chimney Pond for the Park, and the Park Authority allowed me, when I had the time, to operate a burro packing business which brought in an average of $250 a season. Any extra money was always welcome. In addition to that business, we Rangers could sell a few things such as AMC guide books, USGS maps, candy, soda, etc. For my family, that added income was a big help against our winter expenses as our Park job was only seasonal, and the pay wasn't that great.

Roaring Brook

As our time at Baxter passed from the first summer to three summers and then six, and beyond, our memories began to mix and meld. Eddie was growing up, learning to walk one day, fishing beside me the next. We never tired of the changing light and weather on the mountain, but our life in the woods developed a rhythm, and sometimes now it's hard to remember exactly which year various things happened.

Early on, Ralph Dolley, my old friend and the Ranger at Russell Pond, wanted me to start packing in to his camp too, so we spent some time clearing and widening the trail. Bill Tracey, the former owner of the camps at Russell, and another one of the Stacyville Traceys, had used pack horses in past years, so the trail was called the Tracey Pack Horse Trail, and ran almost due north up the valley between Katahdin and Turner Mts. The trail crossed several small streams along the way. If I could hop rocks, I did, and when I couldn't I just waded across in the tennis shoes I usually wore on the trail. After all, tennis shoes dried out after a while. But, the last crossing , the main branch of Wassataquoik Stream, was quite wide with fast- running water, the kind of place to have a sturdy stick to steady yourself on the slippery rocks.

On the burros' first trip they didn't like the small streams, but really balked at going into the Wassataquoik. However, on later trips they remembered that the camp and a feed of oats were only a few more minutes away, and getting them to cross was not a problem. Packing to Russell Pond soon became a regular part of our routine. The trip, about eight miles, took some three to four hours so I usually left in late afternoon then spent the night visiting with Ralph, which we both enjoyed. While the trip was no problem during most seasons, in early spring, high water made crossing the Wassataquoik both miserable and very dangerous.

The bottom corners of the burros' canvas saddle bags became

worn, and Nancy who had a liking for cardboard found that she could turn her head and reach whatever happened to be located at the hole on the front corner. I usually made it a point not to put a carton or box in that spot, but on one trip to Russell Pond, there happened to be a box of Rinso soap powder in the wrong place. Nancy got to it, chewed on the box, and we spread Rinso half way to Russell while she blew soap bubbles. She suffered no effects from that episode, but one thing that did bother both Nancy and Jack was flies, especially the deer and moose flies. I bought Gulf cattle spray to help make their lives less miserable, and when black-flies were thick I even sprayed my clothes. It helped.

I never carried water for myself when packing to Chimney or Russell Ponds, or traveling anywhere in the Park for that matter. While all of the streams and brooks offered good drinking water, there was one spot on the climb to Chimney Pond where I always stopped for a special drink. About three quarters of the way up, the trail skirted some moss-covered ledges where you could hear the water gurgling out of a crack in the rock. At that point the rock was covered with snowberry vines, but by pushing the vines apart and getting down on my knees, I could get my lips to a flow of the cold-est, sweetest water I have ever found. If the snowberries were ripe and white, I enjoyed the special minty flavor of a few, before fin-ishing the climb with a lighter step.

As that game warden had warned me, bears did become a prob-lem. One night as I lay in bed watching lightning flashes and lis-tening to the crash of thunder during a steady rainstorm, a car horn started blowing. It kept on and on. Surely, I thought someone will do something about it. But no, it didn't stop, it just got more and more annoying. I got up, dressed, put on a raincoat, and went out to locate the car which I quickly found in the parking lot. The first thing I noticed was that the window on the passenger side was gone, so I soon figured out what had happened. Those people had gone up to Chimney Pond leaving behind some food on the floor behind the driver's seat of their two-door sedan in which the front seats were hinged.

The second thing I noticed was that the smell of a wet bear was very heavy. The people must have left the window down a bit, just enough for Mr. Bear to get his claws into the top and rip it out. After he got inside, when he went into the back seat to get at the food, he had pushed the seat forward onto the horn. The sudden, loud noise must have spooked him, and I'd say he probably left back out that window in a hurry, because the upholstery was considerably torn. Picturing what had happened I had to laugh, but what would the owners think? Well, when they came down the next day they were not a bit upset. What a story they had to tell when they got home.

Bears weren't the only scavengers who liked to visit camp. Our trash receptacles were 55-gallon barrels placed around the area, and of course they were pretty tempting to the bears and raccoons. I tried emptying the cans late in the day, then used heavy rubber straps to hold the covers on, but you can't outsmart those animals. Whenever we knew bears were around, of course we warned people not to leave food where it would be a temptation, and while most campers were very careful, we did occasionally get campers who were somewhat careless, thinking it would be "exciting" to see a bear.

One time, we'd been hearing some reports from campers of a bear hanging around the area at night, where the campers were meeting it on the way to the outhouse. One man came to me with his story. He and family were sleeping in one of the open-front lean-to's, when a "huge" bear came up and put his front feet on the edge of the floor and looked in at them. The bear backed away when the man sat up, but then that bear picked up their cooler and smashed it against a rock to get the contents. Clearly, this was a creature to be avoided.

Mary Jane almost bumped into it one night coming back from the outhouse, then a night or two later, what was probably the same bear slashed a tent. The party had hiked in to Russell Pond for a night, and while they had put their food away, they'd left an unwashed fry pan in the tent. The grease in that pan tasted pretty good to Mr. Bear. I wondered where we'd see him the next, but thankfully he decided to move on.

Sometimes scientists got permission to collect specimens such as plants, insects, even small animals in the Park. Studying voles, a rodent similar to a mouse, a couple from out of state arranged to tent for two weeks to trap the voles. They seemed like a nice couple, but as they preferred to be off by themselves, I put them on a tent site farthest from the rest of the sites. Every day, they climbed the mountain checking the traps, then in the late afternoon and evening, they worked at stretching the hides and preparing their specimens. We got to know them a little and they were pleasant people. She had prepared food to last most of their stay, and the home-baked bread, cakes, hams, and cured meats were stored in a large box that fit across the bed of their pickup truck. One afternoon he came to the office all excited and asked me to come down to see what a bear had done to their supplies. The storage box was on the ground with the cover open, and that box was practically empty. The bear fortunately had not bothered the tent, but they were pretty upset, and wanted to know if the Park would do anything about their losses.

I phoned Helon and he came right up. After helping to calm the couple, he suggested it was time to get rid of that bear. While we were standing there discussing just that, I heard the bear in the woods not over a hundred feet from us. Helon nodded, so I hurried up to camp to get my rifle. Quickly returning, rifle in hand, I stood with the others for several minutes listening, then I took a few steps into the woods. I heard the bear start to move, and then saw him heading toward the brook. I had a good chance for a shot and fired. He kept right on going, fast. I looked at Helon, telling him quietly, " I know I hit him." I reloaded and we followed his trail carefully.

"Here he is," Helon said a short time later. The bear was dead. Later I checked the spot where we had first heard him in the woods, and I found a half dozen smashed coolers he had stolen from campers. I think Helon made some kind of arrangement to repay the couple for their losses, and it wouldn't surprise me if he paid them out of his own pocket.

The bear's coat looked to be in pretty good condition, so I decided MJ and I ought to have a bear skin rug. Helon helped me get the animal up to the woodshed where we planned to skin it the next day, but just as we hung it up, the scientist came running up. He wanted a chance to inspect it first, looking for parasites. Well, we got it " scun" out as Helon said, and I carefully salted the pelt and rolled it up to take care of later. Yup, you guessed it...I never did get around to it.

The only time I met a bear on the trail was on a packing trip in to Russell Pond. The burros and I had crossed Wassataquoik Stream and were going upstream through the New City clearing. Being much more than halfway along on the trip, I was just walking along with the burros following me when a large bear stood up just off the trail to my left. The burros got skittery, so I took hold of their lead ropes, trying to decide what to do next. About that time I noticed two small cubs to the right climbing a tree. We were between them and their mother which is not a good place to be. Nancy's ears were laid back, but the burros did not freak, and we just continued to move along slowly while I kept a wary eye on mother.

A mother bear and two very small cubs made a few nightly visits to our trash barrel one spring, then later in the summer one of the cubs, partly grown, started prowling the campground, even during the day. Again, thinking that feeding and seeing a bear would be exciting, campers were putting out food for him in spite of my warnings that he would become a nuisance, and dangerous. Finally he left, but he showed up again in the fall, and he wasn't small anymore.

Two young men arrived that fall and were assigned a lean-to at the lower end of the area. A little later one of the fellows came to the office and informed me that a bear was bothering them. "We were trying to have our lunch and the bear climbed right up on the table."

"Is the bear there now?" I asked.

"No, but it's still around, we can hear it in the bushes."

I suggested they move to a different lean-to closer to the office as there were no other parties in the campground at the time. A half hour later the man was back at the office. "We're leaving. We can't even get our stuff packed. The bear climbed right in the trunk." I drove my truck to their lean-to and blew the horn to chase the bear away while they finished packing. I offered to give them a refund, but, well, they seemed to be in a hurry to go.

Life at Roaring Brook was good for MJ, Eddie, and me. We gradually got more modern conveniences, making life easier than it has been at any other of our camp-homes. Besides the Coleman stove, we now had a Coleman pressing iron, lamps, and a lantern. Next I bought a used washing machine with a small gasoline engine mounted underneath. No more hand washing, a relief even though the washing machine was cranky and hard to start most of the time. After another year we got the bright idea of piping water from the brook. Helon found enough money in the budget to buy the pipe, and we went upstream a ways and laid two lengths of two-inch galvanized pipe in the water. By gradually reducing the size of the piping, we had a three-quarter inch pipe into the kitchen, with a tap outside the camp. When that seemed to work OK, we extended the line, running a branch down to the tenting area.

Our next improvement was to put a tee in the three-quarter inch line where it ran alongside the garage so we could pipe water up to a steel barrel supported by a wood frame. This became a shower, and although the water never did get especially warm, it still felt pretty good on a real hot day.

Spring and fall were times for the crew to work together on Park projects. In the spring of '52, one of the repair jobs was the swinging bridge at Katahdin Falls. The bridge, a half mile or so up the Hunt Trail was made of wood planking supported by steel cables, and the planks needed replacing. Helon asked me if I could pack the material to the site with the burros. I said we could sure try, but I decided to just use Nancy. She was more rugged, and I figured Jack would balk at such strange loads. As soon as the roads were passable I moved Nancy, to the Katahdin Stream campground. I had to make some adjustments to her pack saddle in order

115

to tie on the loads, pieces of heavy, green 2x6 plank, each about 40 inches long. We made nine trips over a period of three days, carrying a little over 100 pieces. The planking made for an awkward load compared to her usual saddle bags, but she got the tough job done, and we got the bridge repaired.

A spring ritual that we Rangers enjoyed was the annual woodcock count which Helon did for Fish and Wildlife. For a short period in April the male birds put on a show worth watching and hearing, and because Helon couldn't seem to hear the song of the courting male, he enlisted any of us willing to help. In the early evening he drove us over to the west side of the Park where there were several small clearings along the Park road, beside Sourdnahunk Stream. Woodcocks could usually be found in those clearings, so Helon would drive to those spots, park, and turn off the engine. Soon we heard the "peent, peent" of the male bird. If the light was right we might even see him strutting around on the ground. Then he would take off on a flight that spiraled upward, circling the area for a minute or two where the unseen female, one for each signing male, sat on the ground. The flutter of his wings would end as he floated down to the exact spot he had taken off from. It was a beautiful sight in the early evening light. And, too, we always saw moose, deer, and other animals on those trips.

I loved to look at old maps, and whenever I could find the time I explored the nearby area trying to match the maps I'd studied. Climbing up through the woods from the parking lot one day I came to an outcrop of rock where I could look down on my campground. I could also see what looked like a clearing just beyond Roaring Brook, a spot named on the map as Caribou Bog. It certainly looked intriguing, so one day I crossed the brook and struggled through thick growth for about a quarter of a mile to reach it. The bog covered several acres and was very interesting with bog cranberries, and high bush blueberries in spots around the edge, but most interesting was an abundance of the insect-eating pitcher plant. I watched as bugs became trapped on the sticky surface on the inside of the leaf, becoming food for the plant. Fascinating.

Pleased by what I had discovered, I thought that the bog could be an added attraction for visitors who might want to explore it too, so I gradually opened up and marked a trail to it.

Another place that aroused my curiosity was "old lumber camp #6" as labeled on a map, near the south base of Turner Mt. I was able to follow a grown-up old woods road from Sandy Stream Pond to where I found the remains of a building, not much of it left. I uncovered parts of an old cookstove whose cast iron door was embossed with the state seal and the word 'Dirigo,' and I wondered how long it had been since the stove had seen use. There were a few axe heads, none worth salvaging, but I did lug that stove door home where I managed to chisel out the seal and 'Dirigo' for souvenirs. There were other abandoned small settlements in the woods too, and while working on the trail to Russell Pond with Ralph Dolley, we had found some of those other sites, places that readily gave up rusted tools and memories of the lumbering days.

South Turner Mt. rose sharply from the shores of Sandy Stream Pond, and Superintendent Taylor approved a decision to build a trail to the summit. Dolley and I surveyed and spotted the trail in the spring then a crew from the Appalachian Mt. Club came later to clear and mark it. Ben Hatch, a member of the Club, brought me his odometer-mounted bicycle wheel so I could measure the trail, and he asked me to write a description for the Club trail book, which I did.

The view in all directions from the top of the new trail was great but to the west, across the valley, Katahdin's peaks rose 2000' above hikers, offering terrific views of the Great Basin, the North and Little North Basins. Beyond and a little north of Katahdin, The Brothers and Mullen Mt. showed their heads, then swinging around the compass, you had beautiful Wassataquoik Lake and Webster Lake in the distance. Continuing around the compass, next was Pogy, South Branch, and the Traveler Mts. In the northeast, Mt. Chase's sharp peak seemed to stand alone. Looking to the east over Daicey Mt and the Penobscot East Branch valley, the farmlands added their patchwork pattern to the picture.

117

Southerly lay Millinocket Lake and the widespread waters of the West Branch of the Penobscot River. The stacks of the paper mill in Millinocket were visible over a ridge, and Mattamiscontis, Ragged, and Joe-Mary Mts. could be seen in the distance. The top of South Turner Mt. offered a gorgeous panorama, well worth the climb.

Roaring Brook Campground seemed to attract more visitors each year, and was becoming one of the busiest spots in the park. In addition to our campers, all the traffic to Chimney and Russell Ponds still passed through, and most of them checked in with us both on their way in and again when returning. Day use, picnicking, and sightseeing had increased also.

As public use and the popularity of the Park grew, the need for more facilities became clear. Originally, three six-man and three two-man lean-to's had been built on a fairly level area along the bank of Roaring Brook. I suggested to Helon that we could put two more upstream, but still within the boundaries of the campground. He liked the idea responding, "Go ahead and clear the sites, and I'll get the money for lumber." .

Well, a huge tree stump right in the center of one site presented quite a problem. Now, I don't know where he got it, but Helon brought me some dynamite, caps, and fuse. I had never used dynamite, but I had seen the process somewhere, and figured I could do it. On a late fall day when no one was around I got down to business. I'll have to admit I was a little nervous. I poked a deep hole under the stump with a bar, put a cap on the end of a piece of fuse which I hoped was long enough, and pushed the fuse very carefully into the end of a stick of dynamite. Then I shoved it down into the hole . I took a deep breath, stood back, and surveyed the situation. It's OK, I surmised. Taking a last look around to be sure nobody was nearby, I lit the fuse, and ran up the hill a ways. WHOOMP! A dull explosion shook the ground a little sending some debris flying, but it worked. It worked!

I was able to pull the large pieces of that stump out with the truck and a long cable, and soon the site was ready. We had decided on a four-man size for all new lean-to's. Now, building those lean-to's and outhouses started with going down the road a few miles to where a cedar swamp, not too far from the road, supplied logs for the sills. Small logs I could lug out on my shoulder, but the long ones for building a lean-to required help, not always available right when needed. I liked working with an axe, hewing the top surface flat, and notching the ends for a good fit. It was satisfying work, and I finished those two lean-to's, and then over the next few years, built three more on the downstream end of the camping area.

Governor Baxter came on his annual visit while I was working on one of the lean-to's. He wanted to see the work in progress so he and the group traveling with him came down to where I was nailing log siding on an almost-finished shelter. After admiring the building he remarked, " I'd like to drive a nail so I can say I helped build a lean-to." I started a nail well into the wood then handed him the hammer. He did a good job of it. "There," he said, and everyone applauded. He really seemed quite pleased with his accomplishment.

Two new campgrounds were built in the north end of the Park at South Branch Pond and Sourdnahunk Field, adding two more Rangers to the Park crew. All the Rangers, except Ralph Dolley were married, and the wives you might say were unpaid employees. When the Ranger was not in the office, doing outside work or away for any reason, his wife met the public, registered the campers and talked with them. They filled a need without complaining, and while the wives weren't paid, they were certainly appreciated.

Fires and Rescues

One spring evening in the early 50s when the crew was staying with Helon at Park Headquarters at Togue Pond, a call came in from the Forest Service patrolman stationed nearby. There was a fire burning just south of the road to Greenville, and he needed help. After filling with water and loading some backpack tank pumps, shovels and other firefighting tools in the truck, we caught up with the patrolman and followed him to the fire, easy to spot as the sky shone red ahead of us in the increasing darkness. It was just a ground fire, burning in an area that had burned before, years earlier. However, the wind was blowing quite hard so our job was to keep the fire from spreading until a fire crew arrived. We were working hard, hot and sweaty, when, of all things, it started to snow. Not just a few flakes, it was a spring snow squall blown in by a cold north wind. I certainly wasn't dressed for that kind of weather and welcomed the arrival of the Forest Service crew from Millinocket with more manpower and equipment. Imagine... fighting a fire in a snowstorm.

The Forest Service patrolman's station was at Togue Pond, not far from Park HQ, so he frequently called on park personnel for firefighting help. Another time he needed help on a fire at Rum Brook on the road between Togue Pond and Roaring Brook camp. I met the patrolman at the site where we discovered that a fisherman had left a lunch fire which had begun to spread into the woods. Thankfully, it had been reported early enough so it was easy to contain. I'm not sure of the statistics, but many fires were started by careless campers, as well as by lightning.

A few years later on a nice, sunny summer morning, quiet and peaceful, I smelled smoke as I walked up to the outhouse. Wait a minute, that's not the usual campfire odor, I realized. Walking down toward the camping area I lost the smell, so I headed back uphill to camp until I picked it up again. The wind was coming from the south, from the direction of Togue Pond. I called Helon on my recently acquired radio, but he knew of no fire and there was no smell of smoke at Headquarters. " Well, I think there is a fire between you and me. I'll check and call you back."

Grabbing my trusty axe, I went down to the parking area where I had recently marked a trail heading up the mountain toward Pamola Peak. About a quarter mile up that trail, there was an out-crop of rock with a nice view to the east overlooking my Roaring Brook campground. I figured I might spot any fire from the look-out, but that morning, before I even got to the lookout, the smell of smoke coming from the south was so strong, I just followed the smell. After a half to three-quarters of a mile I found the smoke source, and it was pretty strange. A birch tree, with roots straddling a large boulder, had been struck by lightning which then ran down the tree roots into the ground where the fire was burning deep in the duff, the accumulation of years of decay, under the surface. There had been no storm for over a week that I could remember, so that fire had been smoldering for quite a while.

I had been traveling parallel to the road, so I just headed down-hill, spotting a trail on the way until I hit the road. Back at camp, I quickly called Helon who notified the Forest Service while I filled an Indian tank pump and loaded it in my truck. My son Eddie, who was about five years old at that time, was very mindful that he was the Park Ranger's son, something he took quite seriously. He min-gled with the campers, showed them how to build a campfire, made sure they washed dishes downstream, and even picked up their trash. So, as I put two more pumps by the outside water tap, I care-fully instructed Eddie: "Tell any man who comes by that your father the Ranger needs help with a fire and to go down the road to where the truck would be parked, then follow a spotted trail up to the fire." He soon succeeded in sending one man on to help me, but the fire was definitely going to take more water than we could lug up that hill. Pretty soon, the Forestry crew arrived with a tank truck, then set up a relay system with a portable holding tank and gasoline pump half way up to the fire site. It took them the rest of the day digging out the smoldering duff and wetting down the area before they considered that fire out. At the end of that long day, I headed back to camp to thank my little helper and the camper he had recruited.

Aside from our fire duties, as Rangers we also had the authority to enforce Fish and Game laws, which led to some interesting situations. Early one June Sunday, I saw two men and a boy go by the camp carrying a canoe and fishing rods, obviously headed for Sandy Stream Pond. By late afternoon when I had not noticed them come back, I took a walk over to the pond, and met them on their way out. I had a hunch as I casually asked, "How was the fishing?"

" Pretty Good," one of the men answered.

"Well, let's see what you have."

They showed me a creel with fifteen trout in it. Now, five fish per person per day was the limit so they were okay on that, but some of those fish looked a little smaller than the six inch minimum required. Hmmmm. Then I noticed that the boy was sort of hanging back, his basket set on the ground. I made my way toward him. "Let's see what we have here," I motioned toward his creel. Oh boy, more trout !

"Sorry, fellas, but I'll need your licenses," I sighed as I confiscated the trout, telling them they would be contacted by the Warden. Back at camp I emptied the creels into the kitchen sink. Thirty-eight trout, and twenty of the them undersize. The men paid quite a price and too, they never got to taste those fine fish. Even though the Warden let me have the trout and they certainly didn't go to waste, that kind of taking still seemed a shame.

Of course in addition to the fires and the law enforcement we Rangers also attended to minor accidents at our campgrounds, things such as sprained ankles, cuts and bruises. One day, the Chimney Pond Ranger called to say he had a girl with a painfully swollen ankle, and we both knew that getting enough help that day to carry her down would take time. As I was told she wasn't a very big person, I offered to bring her down on Nancy, a plan to which the girl agreed. I put some padding on the pack saddle to make it as comfortable as possible and headed for Chimney Pond where we soon had the girl atop Nancy. Although we came down very slowly, trying to minimize the bumps as much as we possibly could, it was a rough trip for that poor girl, and I could see tears on her cheeks at times.

Although there was very little winter activity in the Park at that time, March of 1951 saw a serious situation develop, one that could easily have become tragic. Perry Greene, who raised Chinook sled dogs, was at Chimney Pond with some Boy Scouts attempting to get a sled team to Baxter Peak, when they learned that a group of students from New Hampshire was in trouble on the mountain. Weather was poor and snow conditions bad when the students started a snow slide on the Saddle trail, and they were roughed up pretty badly. One of the group had fallen on his sharp, pointed ice ax which pierced his thigh. The boys scouts set out to help.

Finding the students, one of the boy scouts with advanced first-aid training quickly treated the axe wound, then the young man was placed on a dog sled to be moved down the mountain. After a brief rest at Roaring Brook camp, the scouts and wounded student continued on by dog sled to Togue Pond where a car was waiting to take the student to Millinocket hospital. The student recovered well, but as a result of that incident we acquired a metal basket litter.

Early that following summer, the basket was hanging in the garage at Roaring Brook when another accident occurred, and the litter came in handy. About six p.m. one Saturday, a call came from Chimney Pond that a girl had fallen on the Knife Edge near Pamola Peak, and she was in bad shape. After getting the litter out of the garage I glanced at Nancy who was contentedly munching on some hay while tied to a tree by the woodshed. I figured that the quickest way to get the litter up to Chimney Pond would be on her back. We had already made the six-plus mile round trip once that day, but packing two trips a day wasn't unusual, and she looked rested. Tying the litter on to the pack saddle took some doing, and because of its length there was no way I could keep it from bumping

123

Nancy's head and her rump as we climbed. She seemed to sense the urgency of the situation because in spite of the discomfort, we made record time, just about one hour. Lil, the wife of the Chimney Pond Ranger, said Andy was up there with the girl along with the nurse from the Girl Scouts' Camp Natarswi , who had arrived at the site with first aid equipment and morphine. Leaving Nancy tethered at Chimney Pond I moved on. Although I found two men to help get the litter up the Dudley trail, it was still a hard climb, and it was getting dark.

I took the lead end of the litter, one man on the back while the other fellow carried the flashlight, the two of them taking turns on the carry. Traveling the Knife Edge isn't easy at any time, but at night there were even more challenges. It must have been near midnight when we arrived at our destination and lowered the basket down about 50' to where the girl lay on a ledge. She had been lucky; if the ledge hadn't stopped her fall she would have dropped another 100', or more. Our part was over for the moment, and my helpers and I were bushed.

There was not much room on the ledge so the crew had to be very careful getting the girl securely strapped into the basket. Then came the agonizing job of inching the loaded litter up to the trail. That wonderful nurse, who had been on the ledge for hours by then, stayed right by the girl's side the whole time making sure she was as comfortable as possible. It seemed like hours before the litter and its occupant was finally at the top. By then, word had spread on the mountain and more help had arrived, so we were able to take turns carrying the injured girl down. The rocky trail made for very difficult going, especially as the beam of a flashlight was not always aimed where it did the most good. As daylight came the going became easier.

About 6 a.m., we arrived at Chimney Pond, where Lil had coffee and food ready. All of us were grateful not only for the hot food, but that another crew was there waiting to carry the girl the rest of the way to a waiting ambulance at Roaring Brook. After a welcome respite, I wearily rubbed Nancy's forehead thanking her for her help, then we headed for home. It had been a long tense night, but thanks to the efforts of many folks, a very successful rescue mission.

Aside from a drama such as that rescue, life was usually busy, but calm.

One family we had met became our good friends, often coming to picnic with us on weekends. Bob Mott, who worked at the paper mill in Millinocket, liked being in the woods whenever possible. We enjoyed the whole family, which included his wife and two children, as they were always fun to be with especially Bob who liked to play practical jokes. One Sunday he showed up with an old bed spring which he proceeded to carry across the brook and into the woods about a hundred yards. Next he nailed something to a tree on the far side of the stream. It was a sign reading "SPRING" with an arrow pointing into the woods. I don't know if anyone fell for the ruse, but I let him enjoy his joke for a week or two, before taking down the sign.

Bob kept a small plane, a Piper Cub, at the Millinocket airport and asked me if I'd like to see what Katahdin looked like from the air. Would I! I jumped at the chance and not too long after that, we were cruising over the mountain at about 6500'. WOW! That bird's eye view of the country with its seemingly endless forests also showed me the mountain and its basins from an entirely new perspective. Bob circled the mountain, my Katahdin, several times so I could see its beauty and ruggedness from all angles. We were right over Baxter Peak, then we were flying the length of the Knife Edge, the views just stunning. His Piper Cub had a hinged drop-down door on the passenger side which Bob suggested I open so I could take pictures with my new camera. Oh my gosh! I was glad I was well strapped in as the whole side of the plane was open. Losing altitude on our final circle, we were looking right into the Great Basin and Chimney Pond. I was awed.

"Want to get a closer look?" Bob asked. Sure, I nodded without a thought. The next moment Bob made a steep banking circle right inside the basin just below the altitude of Baxter Peak. I could hardly believe what we were doing, but as we came out of the basin and leveled off, I started breathing again. What a thrill, and so unexpected. Back at the airport, I thanked Bob for a great flight, the first of many more hours I would spend in the air with him.

Campers and Climbers

Campers and climbers can be interesting people, and we saw a wide range of folks every summer in the Park. One year, a family with several children tented for two weeks at Roaring Brook. One of the children, a boy about eight years old, had a thing about snakes, so we called him "the snake boy." He loved to catch snakes would carry one around, holding the snake just behind the head. I'm sure some of the other campers steered clear of him, especially the day he came up to the office with six snakes dangling from his fingers. "Where'd you find all those snakes?" I asked.

"Your woodpile's full of them," he answered, adding, "I'm going put them back so I can catch them again." I went out to watch him turn them loose, listening to him talk about how nice snakes are, " not slimy like some people think. Here," he offered as he held one out to me. I had never held a snake before and can't say as I wanted to then either, but I just couldn't refuse such an offer from a little boy. Even though I didn't enjoy the feeling of that squirming reptile, it wasn't too bad, although handling snakes never did become a habit with me.

And then there was the man who set up a battery operated record player in his lean-to, which was a bit unusual. He put on a recording of the sounds of a train, the whistle blowing, the clackety-clack of the wheels, all the noises of a speeding train. Turning up the volume so everyone in the campground could hear it, he soon had a gathering of curious campers at his lean-to, leading to some interesting comments from folks stopping by our office. Now I preferred the sound of the wind in the trees, but I learned that the man was in the electronics business, and had built the machine for Ranger Dolley at Russell Pond as Ralph liked music and had lots of records, but no way to play them. The next time I packed a party in to Russell and spent the night, I was awakened to the lovely voice of Doris Day singing "Bewitched, Bothered and Bewildered" and

"My Secret Love," both vastly preferable to train whistles in the woods.

One of the most interesting persons I met on the mountain, one who also became a very good friend, was Maurice "Jake" Day from Damariscotta, Me. He had organized a group of a half dozen or so of his friends, and the group, which came to be known as "Jake's Rangers," made frequent sojourns to the North Country, and particularly to Baxter Park. Jake also had a camping buddy named Lester "Sawdust" Hall, and together, Jake and Lester had explored and knew more about the Park than anyone I had met. Hall had made his first trip to Chimney Pond in 1929. On one occasion they boiled a pail of tea while having lunch on a large boulder on the shore of Sandy Stream Pond. Jake ever after referred to that boulder as "Pinch-o-Tea Rock." I got to know them as I packed gear for them a number of times to Chimney and Russell Ponds. One day while Jake and Hall were camping at Roaring Brook, the three of us were looking at the topographical map of the Park in my office, when Jake pointed to some ponds on the east side of South Turner Mt. mentioning that he'd always wanted to see those ponds. Well I had fished the larger of the two ponds, and had reached them both by skirting the south slope of Turner Mt. There were no trails to the area and it could be rough going in places, but I agreed to take them in after the heavy use season was over.

At that time, Jake was close to 70 years old, and Lester well over 70, something I was aware of, but not especially uneasy about. I knew both men were rugged and savvy, plus we planned to camp for one night, and travel as light as possible. It was the last week the Park was open in October when we made the trip, and the rich foliage color added a lot to our enjoyment of the occasion. I decided we'd take advantage of the new trail up to the summit of South Turner, then head north across the saddle between the South and North peaks. Jake was an avid photographer and wanted to document the trip on film, so that would be the most scenic approach to the ponds. It was a perfect fall day, no rain in the forecast, clean, crisp air and great visibility. The climb up Turner went quite slowly, and I could see that it was going to take longer than I had planned. Not that those two fellas couldn't keep pace, but it seemed every time we stopped, Jake would be putting new film in his camera.

At the summit we spent a long time enjoying the magnificent view before Jake got out his binoculars. "Look," he said, pointing a fair way off, "there's a moose in Sandy Stream Pond." It was time to move on as we still had a ways to go yet before we reached the ponds. All downhill now from the summit, but still slow going through thick growth at times. There were signs of moose having yarded up here in the previous winter, places where the scrub growth had been browsed heavily. Finally we reached a point where we could look down on the ponds. We angled down through stands of shining white birch in the general direction of the ponds, and finally came out on the shore of the upper pond which set in a small basin against a steep rock wall. Hardly a ripple on the water, and the afternoon sun highlighted the brilliant reds and bright yellows of the foliage around the pond. A really beautiful place in the wilderness of Baxter Park. It had taken us about eight hours to get there, but we all agreed it was worth the effort.

Time to pick a spot for our campsite. Part of the plan was to have a mess of trout for supper, so while Jake and Lester set up camp and built a fire, I put my fly rod together and scouted a good spot to cast a fly. Fortunately the trout were hungry, and I soon had enough brightly colored, native brook trout for our supper. Lester did the honors of cooking those trout, and he did a great job. Well nourished and enjoying our pipes by the campfire, we drank a toast or two to old Pamola who just might be looking down on us from the Knife Edge. It was a moonless night leaving the sky crowded with a myriad of glowing stars. Lying in my sleeping bag later I thought: What could be better than this?

Another time, the whole group of Jake's Rangers came to the Park planning to climb to Chimney Pond their first day, and then the next day hike in to Russell Pond, and eventually on to South Branch Pond, making the trip through the Park from south to north.

129

They would try the fishing at Russell and other ponds all along their way. The group, which included a renowned guest, Supreme Court Justice William O. Douglas, arrived at Roaring Brook, checked into the bunkhouse, and invited me to have supper with them. I was pretty well acquainted with Jake and most of the Rangers, and thoroughly enjoyed being with them and Justice Douglas, who was well regarded as a woodsman.

After supper a bottle of Irish whisky was passed around, and before long, stories of past fishing trips dominated the conversation, with the fish getting bigger and bigger as the evening progressed. At some point I noticed that Douglas was the only person in the room not smoking. It seemed unusual, so I asked him if he had ever been a smoker. " Oh, yes," he answered, "I was a heavy smoker for many years." He went on to describe how difficult it had been to quit, but how each day the desire for a cigarette had become less and less.

Soon after that conversation, I excused myself to go back to camp for my nightly radio sign off. When I called the Forest Service in Millinocket, I was told that the press had heard Douglas was here, and a reporter wanted to know if Justice Douglas would have a few words to say for them. Back to the bunkhouse I went. "Of course we can do that, get me a piece of paper to write on," offered Douglas. No one could produce any paper so Justice Douglas tore a piece from a cookie box and scribbled, "I have known Katahdin for over a quarter century. It is for me my favorite mountain the world around. It is not high as mountains go, but one who looks up for four or five thousand feet to see the clouds playing over it sees a mountain peak in all its splendor. There are trails to climb, cliffs to scale, meadows to explore, and lakes to fish. Moose, deer and bear adorn the area. This is a place for quiet relaxation and soul searching." A local newspaper featured his words in a write-up a few days later.

That night, I thought about how beautiful and inspiring his words were, and before I turned in, I said to myself, " If he can do it, I can." I quit. What cigarettes I had, I burned in the stove, and I never smoked again.

Groups from boys' and girls' camps made up a large part of the Park's public use. For the most part the campers were a pleasure to work with, but sometimes they could be a problem and the rules and regulations were bent a little. It seemed that all little boys must have a hatchet, and they just must try it out on a tree, and the bark of a white birch peels off so nicely. Sometimes the wash area downstream was too far to walk to, and, when it was raining, well, why not chop wood on the sill log inside the lean-to. Sometimes the miscreant was a counselor, and I still have the notes I wrote down on this particular one.

The counselor was alone, in charge of fourteen boys, and it was raining. He made frequent trips up to the office with his questions and problems: "How can we get firewood? We can't build a fire." The next visit, " We have steak, how are we going to cook it? Can we rent a stove?" And again, "I'm getting wet, do you have a pair of boots I can borrow? What if the boys get pneumonia?"

I guess he managed to get supper somehow before he came up to the office that evening to tell me they were packing up to Chimney Pond in the morning, and planned to climb the mountain. As he turned to leave, he casually added, "I don't know if they can make it or not, most of the boys have never done anything even approaching this. I can hardly wait to see their sweaty faces." I could hardly believe what I was hearing. But, sure enough, he sent a group of boys off in the morning on their climb to Chimney Pond, without a counselor. I called ahead to warn the Ranger of possible trouble, but those boys were fortunately able to complete their trip without mishap, to my great relief and quite probably to that counselor's great chagrin.

Finally, We Run a Sporting Camp

Even though I had a good job with the Park, MJ's and my original idea of owning a Sporting Camp certainly hadn't been forgotten, and again it was Leon Crommett who came to us with a possibility. The Cedar Lake camps which we had seen earlier had been bought and were being operated by a man from Millinocket, who was looking for someone to go in that fall and run the business during hunting season. Crommett brought him to see us and talk over the arrangement. We could move in and operate the camp for the hunting season and not have to pay him anything. He assured us some of his sports would be coming back. Sounded like a good deal, then the truth came out.

Apparently many of the deer killed in previous years had been shot between the eyes, and very likely the Game Warden would be watching the camp closely. Night hunting? It seemed the owner couldn't trust himself to run a clean season. He assured us the camp was ready to go, all we had to do was stock up on food. It was a strange situation, but tempting. After considerable discussion, we decided to give it a go, even though caring for a two-year-old might complicate things at times. I knew M.J. could handle the cooking, and I would help in the kitchen and with other chores.

It seemed a good idea for me to have a guide's license, so I contacted the local warden, whose eyes seemed to harden a little when I explained that we'd be running the Cedar Lake camps. But after answering a set of questions and paying a fee, I became a licensed Maine guide. Soon after the Park closed that fall, we did some basic shopping and got ready to move in to Cedar Lake.

While income from the burro packing had continued to add to our income each summer, after a year or two I lost Jack #2, who died while wintering at the farm so from then on good old Nancy did all the work. I really became quite attached to her. To go in to Cedar Lake, I loaded my faithful Nancy into the our pickup truck and we drove to the trail head leading to the camp. Our "wangan" filled both Nancy's saddle bags, and Eddie rode in my pack basket. The weather was nice, Nancy behaved well, and MJ and I enjoyed the three mile walk. It took us several days of hard work to clean the camp and get organized, and hopefully ready, for business. I studied a map of the area and did some exploring to get familiar with our surroundings. There was some deer sign, so hunting might be pretty good.

Our friend Bob Mott flew in with his pontoon plane, bringing a Millinocket doctor for an evening meal. Our first customers. Mindful of our early experiences at Bowlin Camps with the somewhat scanty meals Mrs. Chapman had served, MJ served them a nice supper with no problems. A party of four who had tentative reservations finally showed up, and we put them in one of the cabins. They only stayed a few days, and didn't really hunt very seriously. The camp owner and a friend came in for a day of hunting and shot a bear. I had no way of knowing for sure, but I suspected they shot the bear in its den. The camp owner, I'll call him John, said he could sell the bear to the operator of a camp on Joe-Mary lake. The next day a small plane landed on the lake and taxied up to our dock. I held a wing tip while a grizzled, fairly old man got out. " I'm Jasper Haynes," he said, adding gruffly, "I've come for the bear, and I can't waste time. One of my pontoons has a leak." I helped him tie the bear on the pontoon that didn't leak so the load would balance, and off he flew. Later, Bob Mott told me he had just recently taught Haynes to fly, and that the man's old plane was held together with bailing wire and tape.

I took advantage of the first snow to do some hunting before closing camp. Within a few hundred yards of camp I came on some fresh tracks. Stooping down for a close look, I raised my eyes to find a large buck standing there looking at me, only fifty feet away. I was in an awkward position, but I managed to get my gun up for a shot. At least we had meat for the winter. A good thing too, as those few parties we'd had were the extent of our business that fall. We had not made any money, but it had been quite an experience.

We had certainly learned a few things about operating a sporting camp, just maybe enough to satisfy that old dream that had brought us to Maine.

As the time came to move out drew nearer, Bob Mott arrived one evening offering to fly MJ and Eddie to Millinocket Lake where I could pick them up. At the landing MJ was so excited about the ride they'd had. "Oh , it was beautiful," she exclaimed. "The full moon filled the sky, and lit up the whole country, and I just love flying!"

1953 - 1955

Three years after our boy was born, we were expecting another addition to our family which meant regular trips to see Dr. Mac in Lincoln once again. Before moving to Roaring Brook that spring, we decided to use some of our savings to have a well drilled at our house in Stacyville. With our growing family, it would be good to have water at the house. Now, one of Prince Tracey's relatives drilled wells, when he felt like it, and needed the money. His old rig was the pile driver type that took time to drill down thru ledge when necessary. I made a deal with him: For $3.00 a foot, he could set up the machine and camp there on the property as long as it took to do the job. No hurry, he had all summer, and I do believe he was there most of the summer. When we moved back in the fall, there was plenty of evidence that he had consumed a large quantity of beer, which I suppose was easier than lugging water. The well was about 150 ft. deep, and the water just great, and the cost a fairly reasonable $420.00. All I had to do was install a hand pump, and no more carrying water!

Meanwhile, our summer had been going well. At the end of the season I counted up 45 packing trips to Chimney Pond for the burros and me, giving us extra income that would come in handy. The Park was becoming more popular, and we were busier than ever. Governor Baxter, who made a point of visiting the Park every summer, always enjoyed talking with the Rangers and their families. In one conversation with four-year-old Edward, Mr. Baxter learned that Eddie liked oranges, so after that a bag of oranges became a regular gift from the Governor.

Around the middle of October, MJ, by that time eight months along, began packing a bag with the things she would need at the hospital. Ralph Dolley moved out from Russell to stay with us and brought us a treat of some mountain cranberries. MJ was right in the middle of cooking cranberry sauce one evening when she suddenly turned to us and announced, "It's time to go to Lincoln." We were on the way, leaving Ralph to finish cooking and canning the cranberry sauce, and babysit young Edward.

Again, a long drive with me just hoping to get to the hospital on time. Arriving there late at night, poor Dr. Mac was again dragged out of bed to come in and check on M.J. Hours passed, nothing happened, and by noon the next day the Dr. was telling us it could be another day, so I decided to go back to camp to help take care of Eddie Jr. To help MJ pass the time, Dr. Mac took her over to his home to watch television on his new set, thinking that might help her relax. Finally, the next day, we had a new daughter, and Eddie had a new baby sister, named Catherine. It was time to get the whole family moved back to the house in Staceyville.

The Park was now closed for the season, and Helon moved the crew up to a cabin on Trout Brook where our fall project was to start clearing to build a road in to South Branch Pond where a new campground was planned. I could come home weekends. The cabin was on the other side of Trout Brook from the road so we had to make a temporary single log bridge across the stream. It rained incessantly, and the bridge washed out . We rebuilt it and it washed out again. All in all, we didn't get much work done before our funds, and time, ran out. Now I could go home and cuddle my new daughter.

As usual, work was hard to find that winter. In January I hired on with a crew digging a trench for a pipeline between two buildings at the East Millinocket paper mill. For some reason that I never did understand, that trench had to be hand dug, about six feet deep. A man using a jack hammer broke up the frozen ground ahead of us, and we shoveled up to a platform where another man shoveled to ground level. It was hard work, and I went home dog tired at night. Even though we needed the money I was glad when the job ended.

It was a cold, tough winter, but we got through it. In early spring, Ray Corliss cut some pine logs and dragged them out of the woods. Because they were covered with mud and gravel, the sawmill wouldn't accept them. I took on the messy job of debarking those logs using an axe and a spokeshave, any paycheck always welcome. But, believe me, I was some happy when the day came to start work in the Park again.

That year saw another big improvement in equipping the Ranger Camps, two-way radios. Being surrounded by mountains, the only contacts I had in the Park were Chimney and Russell Ponds and Park Headquarters. However, we were on the Forest Service frequency and could talk with their office in Millinocket from which they were able to relay messages for us. We had been required to log every call we made, a time-consuming chore the new radios would eliminate. Gradually the old telephone lines came down, and no more of the long check-and-repair treks I'd done were needed.

A party of four men checked in early one evening that summer, headed in to Russell Pond for a weekend of fishing. Darkness was coming on quickly, but they had good flashlights and two of them had been in to Russell several times, they said. It was not a good situation, but they were determined to go so I called Dolley on the radio to let him know they were on the way. Somehow they became separated and two of them came back to Roaring Brook about midnight. There was no point in going out looking for the others in the darkness, the weather was good, they had sleeping bags, and their friends felt they would be OK. The two missing men showed up at Roaring Brook early in the morning. They had gotten off the trail, and had decided to bed down and wait for daylight. A smart decision. Of course, they could have just stayed over in the first place.

Avalanche Field, formerly known as Depot Camp, at one time must have been a large grassy area, but had become mostly grown-over with small trees. However, there was still some grass, so I grazed the burros there whenever I could. The field was the starting point of a three mile long tote road in to Cobb's Katahdin Lake Camps. The camp owner had horses he used to pack gear in for his guests, so I guess it was bound to happen. Nancy got loose and went in to Katahdin Lake where she got into the camp barn and

137

helped herself to the supply of oats. The very upset camp owner notified Helon who then called me. When I went to get my burro, I apologized several times to Mr. Cobb, offered to pay for the oats, and promised it wouldn't happen again, but I don't think Mr. Cobb was listening. Nancy was quite content as we headed back to Avalanche Field.

Moose walked through the grounds around Roaring Brook frequently so they were no novelty to us, but the campers got quite excited when one was seen. One night just at dark a man was following a big bull around trying to get a good picture. Somehow he managed to get in front of Mr. Moose for a head-on shot. When the camera's flash went off the moose charged. The man wound up on our front porch, visibly shaken. We never did hear how that picture came out.

Another time, a nice lady, one of a group of teachers, came up to the office. "You told us there were lots of moose around. Well we've been here three days and I haven't seen a moose yet," she complained.

"Look down there by the flagpole, there's your moose."

"Oh, my gosh! I walked right by it. I thought it was one of your donkeys."

Of course that summer was very different from any previous year as we now had two children with us at Roaring Brook, Eddie was three and baby Cathy was less than six months old. Yes it was a very busy time for mother. That summer, M.J. put the playpen on the back porch for Cathy, while Eddie would play nearby. Soon, a curious rabbit came up on the porch and MJ fed it a carrot, ensuring that it would became a regular visitor, for a while at least. On the way to carry water from the brook one day, I got a glimpse of a fisher, and then we didn't see the rabbit after that. In spite of its name, a fisher doesn't eat fish. Although not terribly large, it is a vicious creature, and I had been told that it was the only animal that would tackle a porcupine.

A year or so later, I put up a three-foot high wire fence around part of the yard, and inside that enclosure made a sand box for the

MJ, baby, and bunny

kids. It made a nice, safe play area where MJ could keep an eye on them from the house. Glancing out the window to check Eddie and Cathy one day, MJ saw a curious cow moose, inside the fence, walking up to Cathy in the sand box, the moose's nose right over Cathy's head. MJ froze at the window, holding her breath. Soon the moose ambled off, stepping over the fence as if it wasn't even there. MJ had a story to tell, and I had a fence to raise!

After another wonderful summer on the mountain, we decided to visit family in the fall of 1954. The Stacyville house was pretty well finished with a masonry chimney, and asbestos shingle siding. We had saved enough money to trade the truck for a station wagon, had enough money to travel, and we had a plan.

My father had moved to Phoenix, Arizona about the time we had moved to Maine while MJ's sister Kate and her husband Fred were living in New Hampshire. While I haven't mentioned our families much, we were close in spite of the distances between us. We had kept in touch by letters over the years, and now we were anxious to see them to introduce Eddie and Cathy to them.

We spent Thanksgiving with Kate and Fred, then shared Christmas with our friends Charlie and Bert in Connecticut. Soon

139

after that, we were headed to Indiana where our next stop would be New Year's with my sister Dorothy and her family, and a visit with my brother Marion., or "Toot" as he was being called by then. On the Pennsylvania Turnpike, we had a flat tire and of course the spare was, well, let's just say hard to get to in the jam-cram-packed car, but soon we were rolling into Dorothy's driveway.

After a great visit in Indiana came the long stretch of road to Phoenix. The station wagon was packed full of all the necessary things to take care of two small children ages one and three. On the nights when we stopped at tourist cabins, the crib had to be unloaded then put together, and toys unloaded, too, to keep the little ones happy. By the time we left Indiana where we had spent several days, the children had adjusted to the pack-unpack routine and were good little travelers.

We arrived in Phoenix at six in the morning during a heavy rainstorm, and it never rained again during our three-month stay. The weather was invariably the same, hot every day, but cool at night, quite a change from our previous Maine winters. Dad and his fourth wife Ruth whom we had never met, doted on and spoiled the children while I did some work on the house and grounds. On rides out into the country and desert we saw antelope instead of deer, and road runners rather than partridge. The scenery was beautiful but so dry and arid, so different from Maine.

Phoenix was surrounded by barren sandstone hills, referred to here as mountains, but I saw none that even reminded me of Katahdin and home. My new 35mm camera had recorded much of the scenery, and of course the children and family, to show to the folks back home. As spring approached, the desert cactus was just starting to bloom, and it would have been nice to stay and see the desert in all its glory. We had enjoyed Arizona, but we'd been away from Maine and our mountain for almost three months, and it was time to head home.

Dad had a small camp trailer he wasn't using, so we made a deal. Seems I was always making deals! I could use the trailer for the trip home, then I'd sell it and send him the money. The trip home would make another whole story, but in the end, that deal worked out great for both of us.

It was good to be back home in Maine, but we had some tough decisions to make. Since finding winter work around Stacyville seemed to be getting more difficult each winter, we began to think about a move to Millinocket. It would be nearer the Park, and the children would be starting school before long. I heard of a camp on Smith Pond, a convenient location about three miles out of town on the road to the Park, so we went to see it. It was just a plain typical wood frame camp, three small rooms, electricity, but no plumbing. A hand pump at the kitchen sink brought water from a driven well. It was sparsely furnished, with two wood stoves, one for cooking and the other for heat. We would need the two stoves as the building of course was not insulated.

It sat near the shore of the pond, and from the glassed-in front porch we could see Katahdin. The owner, a very nice elderly lady who lived in town, apparently didn't have use for the camp anymore, and she was asking $2,500 for it. We would just be buying the building as the land was leased from Great Northern Paper Co. for a small yearly fee, but in that location and at that price, it definitely had possibilities.

Meantime the Summit Farm had changed hands, the first of many changes to come. Gerald Merry, the younger brother of the new owner, had become a friend of ours and, having recently married, he was interested in buying our house in the woods. However, in researching my title to the land, I got quite a surprise. I didn't own that land! At the time of my purchase, the Farmer's Home Administration had owned the farm. Finally, after all the strings were untangled, here's the way it worked out: I sold the house to Gerald for $1500 which he would pay to me at $40 a month. At the same time I arranged to buy the camp outside Millinocket, paying for it at $40 a month. Once again, I'd made a good deal.

Yes, after all the work we had put into our little house in the woods, it was hard to say goodbye, and we would miss being close to the many friends who had been so good to us. However, by now we were getting used to change, and I felt sure we could adapt and make new friends.

Winters At Smith Pond

We moved in the fall of 1956, just in time for our son Eddie to start school in Millinocket. Since it was a half mile to the main road and the school bus stop, MJ walked out with him every morning that first year, meeting him again each afternoon too. While the shore of Smith pond was lined with camps, we found that only a few families stayed the winter. One family, the Dionnes, had a tiny store out near the main road, a store mainly for summer business, but they did stay open year round

It seemed I was continually on the road, back and forth from Staceyville to Smith Pond, and still putting in my time in the Park. Of course, I went right to work trying to make a summer camp comfortable for the coming winter. It was still only a camp, but we did have electricity and a telephone. There were no storm windows so I started by covering all the windows on the outside with clear plastic. Since the camp was up off the ground on posts, I banked it with bales of hay to keep some of the cold out. The camp faced northwest across the pond, and we had a good view of Mt. Katahdin but the prevailing wind, fresh and cold off the mountain also came from that direction, and did it blow!

On Christmas Day that first winter it stormed, heavy snow and hard wind which tore the plastic off all the front windows. Our Christmas tree on the glassed in porch had real snow on it, but with two stoves burning, we were able to keep fairly warm. In January it turned very cold, and a severe storm blew down most of the TV antennas in Millinocket, and I was able to find a job for two or three weeks helping to put up new roof antennas. Temperatures fell to -20º, -30º every day, and it seemed the wind would never stop howling. My car wouldn't start most mornings, so I hitchhiked to town, coming home the same way each night, tired and half-frozen.

There were only two other year-round families on our road, and the Great Northern Paper Company plow stopped just past our place, which was good. But then, to add to our winter's problems, the snowdrifts got so high by February, that they stopped plowing altogether. The wind and the cold packed the snow so hard in the road, we didn't even have to use snowshoes. Mary Jane got acquainted with our nearest neighbor, a couple with three young children. The mothers visited back and forth, and Cathy and Eddie had children to play with, something they had missed. Finally in March, Great Northern brought in a bulldozer and opened the road. It was a winter of just surviving the elements.

Winter work in Millinocket did not come as easy as I had hoped. With our second Smith Pond Christmas just a few weeks away and no money coming in, I took on the role of Santa Claus for the town of Millinocket. It required a lot of padding to fill up the suit, but that was good because I had to stand at a makeshift booth out in front of the Post Office for hours in the cold, cold weather. However that Santa stint led to a job that lasted three long winter months, quite a godsend. The owner of the Western Auto store just down the street was going to Florida, so he hired me to work in the store while he and his wife were away. Getting to know more people through that job helped us feel more at home in town, and we were once again feeling fairly settled. Eddie was now in second grade and Cathy just four, so soon enough, she too, would head off to school.

The following winter I got a job at a gas station in town. Now, the owner also had contracts to supply fuel to woods operations, so he had three tank trucks which were kept busy delivering to the woods camps plus making home fuel deliveries in town. In addition to pumping gas at the station, about once a week I drove a truck delivering either gasoline or diesel fuel to one of the woods camps. One camp was on Thistle Pond, some 35 or 40 miles west and north of Millinocket, no quick trip in wintertime. The best part of that trip was having dinner with the logging crew. I usually arrived close to meal time, and a place was always quickly set for me without any asking. Enormous quantities of food disappeared like magic from that table, every bite of it good. No conversation interrupted the job

144

at hand, which was to fill each empty stomach, and no one ever left that table hungry. When the meal was finished these men didn't linger, they got up from the table and went about their business.

Every delivery trip was an experience, certainly not always safe or pleasant either. The roads we traveled were narrow, their snow cover packed hard from trucks hauling pulp wood to the mill in Millinocket. The truck drivers, probably paid by the load, drove as fast as possible, and when I met one coming or going, there was no question who had the right of way. If I had to leave the road to let him pass, and I happened to get stuck, well, someone always came by and pulled my truck back onto the road. Although there were many close calls, I didn't get in any serious trouble until, ironically, the last trip in the spring.

Another driver named York and I were loading our two trucks the night before the trip so we could get an early start. While I was filling my truck, an old Mack, with gasoline, and York was loading fuel oil in his newer vehicle, I asked if he'd mind swapping trucks for the trip. I had usually been stuck with the old, slow, hard-shifting Mack and I wanted to drive the better vehicle, just once. York agreed. In the morning I led off enjoying the newer, quicker, easier-shifting truck, slowing down frequently on the road to let York catch up in the Mack. When I came to the top of a long, steep, downgrade called Abol Hill, York and the Mack were nowhere in sight, so I downshifted and started down slowly. At the bottom of the hill, just as I was stopping to wait for him, I heard his horn blowing, blasting, blaring, right behind me. He had lost his brakes on the hill and in spite of frantic downshifting, he was still coming at a pretty good speed.

That narrow road left little room to pass, and he clipped the rear corner of my truck, which sent his truck into the ditch where it rolled over on its side. A hatch cover loosened, and gasoline started running out. I ran over and climbed up to open the cab door to haul York out. He just looked up at me, cigarette in his mouth, as I hollered, " Put out that *&$%)#@ cigarette and turn off the ignition! Are you alright," I asked almost as an afterthought. Dazed but

145

not hurt, he didn't say a word as I helped him out of the cab. Once on the ground, he quickly regained his presence of mind, ran around to the other side of the truck, closed the hatch, and stopped the flow of gasoline.

After we both caught our breath, we inspected the trucks. We couldn't right the Mack of course, but the damage to my vehicle was minor, and after all, we still had a load of fuel oil to deliver, so York and I climbed into my truck and continued on. Not long after crossing Ripogenus Dam we came to the Levenseller's camps, a spot where I usually stopped to say hello to Boots and his wife , who were always glad to have company. After relating our predicament to them, we borrowed their telephone and called our boss to tell him what had happened. He listened to our story, asking if either of us was hurt, then agreed we should continue our journey. He didn't really say much except "Go ahead and finish your trip." We were soon back on the road to Thistle Pond where we unloaded the fuel, enjoyed a rest and filled up on a snack of coffee and left-over pie from dinner before heading home again.

On the way home we discussed how the boss would react to our accident, the damage to the Mack, and the undelivered load of gasoline. When we reached Abol Hill, we were relieved to see that the overturned truck was gone. It had been righted and towed back to Millinocket, where we found that our boss didn't seem too upset, allowing as how accidents do happen. Soon, that old Mack was back on the road, and one day as York and I stood looking at it, he remarked out of the side of his mouth, "I shoulda' taken a match to it while I had the chance."

Winter Climbing on Katahdin

Ken Wetmore had been talking to me about climbing Katahdin in the winter. We both understood the need for crampons and ice axes for the upper part of the climb, and as he had managed to find some at a surplus store, he called me one winter evening with a plan. Since the road to the Park had not been plowed past Millinocket Lake, we would get Chink Lagasse to fly us in to Katahdin Lake from his base at Millinocket Lake, then we'd snow-shoe the five miles to the camp at Roaring Brook, stay there the night, and climb the mountain next day. Quite a plan.

It sounded good to me and the weather was moderate, so I phoned Lagasse and made arrangements for the flight the next day. Ken arrived at our house, where we double-checked our gear, then picked up a few groceries and were on our way. The flight was uneventful but very beautiful. I had flown over the mountain. in summer, but looking down on Katahdin and the other mountains covered by their blankets of blazing white, that was a spectacular sight. After a nice landing on the snow-covered lake, we strapped on our snowshoes, hoisted backpacks, and headed for camp. I expected to see moose and deer tracks, but apparently with the heavy snows the animals were yarded in sheltered areas near food supplies, and we saw little sign of wildlife. The snowshoeing was good and soon I was building a fire in the stove at Roaring Brook camp, a very familiar experience in an unfamiliar season.

It was exciting to think about what the new day would bring. Again, we carefully checked our gear: snowshoes, ice axes, heavy parkas and mittens, sun goggles that fit close to the face, compass, matches, candy bars. All set. Time to hit the sack. Before sleep came however, my Ranger training took over, and I assessed our situation. We were deep in the woods, no other person within miles of us, no means of communication. But, then I realized that there was no one I'd rather be with than Ken. I admired his abilities and knowledge of the woods, and I drifted off to sleep knowing we'd be fine.

In the morning when we started the climb there were a few clouds over Katahdin, but it looked like a good climbing day for us. Taking turns breaking trail, we made good progress until we paused at the Basin Ponds, where we rested and admired the wintry view. After that, the climb became steeper and the going much harder, but finally we reached Chimney Pond. Gosh, where are the lean-to's? Knowing where they should be, I finally located the top edge of one lean-to's roof. I couldn't believe how deep the snow was. Next we came to the Ranger's camp from which the view would be so familiar to me, but I looked up with fresh awe at the walls of the basin now covered with ice and snow. Water coming out of the ledges on the Pamola side had layered tons of ice on the wall, ice almost as blue as the clear winter sky. Absolutely beautiful. I will forever remember the stunning beauty of that moment, but as we had brought our cameras, I knew it would be nice to have it on film too.

From there we followed a stream bed through the woods until we came out in an open area where the snow almost completely covered whatever trees or other growth lay beneath it. Tree tops that just managed to poke up through the hard-packed snow at the lower edge of the area seemed like a good place to hang our snow-shoes while we strapped the crampons to our boots. We are at the foot of the Saddle Trail which would be the easiest climb to the Tableland, but more clouds were building in, and we knew we'd better get moving. Climb a ways, stop and rest. Not bad though. All the rocks of summer covered with snow, I think that that was the easiest way to climb the mountain. Coming up onto the plateau we headed for the peak. Not much snow there, but the rocks and bushes were covered with hoar frost, a ghostly site. We spoke of Pamola.

Only several hundred feet to go when the snow started, light at first, then harder, and the wind was picking up, too. We couldn't see the peak now, but as long as we went up, we figured we certainly would get there. Pushing on, we reached the pile of rocks marking the highest point, quickly we found the metal tube holding the AMC tablet, hastily signing our names and the date for the records. We turned back. Heading downward, we hurried, following our footprints. They disappeared. The snow had covered them, and now everything was white. Ken's nostrils were white, frost-rimmed. He covered the lower half of his face. We continued cautiously, knowing that on our right was a sharp dropoff, with cornices built up at the edge. It was an especially dangerous place, one we had to stay away from.

Checking our compasses didn't help. For some reason they weren't working very well up there. Figuring the wind was out of the NW, we decided our best bet was to go slowly into the wind while bearing to the left, checking the snow ahead of each step. After a while, edging carefully to our right, we came to a spot where we could see a short way down a slope, but what we were seeing didn't look quite right. A little farther on we came to another gully. Looks like the top of the Saddle Trail we agreed with enormous relief. Just then, the snow let up enough for us to confirm that that was our trail. We kept going with more confidence and soon it stopped snowing, then we reached the level area where we had left our snowshoes. We had made it, but it hadn't been quite the climb we'd planned. Had Pamola been trying to tell us something? One sure thing we learned: Mark your back trail in some way so you can return.

That night, warm by the fire at Roaring Brook once again, we reflected on our day's experience, feeling very thankful to have gotten out of a bad situation. In the morning, with a twenty mile trek ahead of us, we decided to lighten our loads by leaving the ice axes and crampons at camp. The weather for our trip out could not have been better, a bright blue, cloudless sky, the air just cold enough to be vigorous. The snow, still mostly hard-packed in spite of the new covering, was good for snowshoeing, and we made pretty good time, although I will admit that by the time we reached our car at Millinocket Lake, our legs were ready for a long rest.

The following year Ken, three other friends, and I decided to try a different approach for a winter climb of Katahdin. We were able to drive from Stacyville, on a plowed hauling road in to a newly-built bridge across the East Branch of the Penobscot to an operating lumber camp on Moose Pond, from where we could see the mountain, WNW on the compass. Donning our snowshoes and packs we left the lumber camp and headed into the woods, figuring on about eight miles of travel to Roaring Brook campground. There were cutting roads along the way, but they all seemed to turn south, away from our planned direction, the direction that would take us out onto the Roaring Brook Road. Traveling through the woods in the middle of winter is so much different, and so much easier than in summer as the deep snow puts you up over blowdowns, rocks and other obstacles on the ground. That area though was quite hilly and ridge after ridge confronted us, some quite steep. One of our party wore long, narrow, pickerel snowshoes, and had some trouble on the hill climbs where he kept sliding back.

Most of the time as we traveled, the mountain was not visible, but whenever we came to a clearing and could see it, we corrected our course. When we finally came to the road we wanted, some-what south of Avalanche Field, it was almost dark and we still had about three miles to go. The Roaring Brook camp was a welcome sight to five weary travelers, but a fire and some food soon restored us.

In the morning we got an early start in perfect weather. The Tableland was windswept and almost free of snow. We had a wonderful climb, a far more relaxed experience than Ken and I had had the year before. At Baxter Peak we all signed the book, then the cameras came out for picture taking. But on our descent of the Saddle Trail, the snow didn't feel quite right. There was new snow on top of the crust, and it tended to move with each step. There was a good chance we might start a slide, so part way down we decided to try a different area on our right. A careful traverse of about 50 ft. brought us to better conditions, but we still proceeded with caution. It was a relief to get down to fairly level ground, back to our snowshoes and on to Roaring Brook.

The following day we located the tote road to Katahdin Lake. While crossing the lake I turned to look back at the mountain. From this spot it was a picture-perfect sight, and I captured it with my camera, thinking that as I had gotten to know Katahdin better and in all seasons, its call had only gotten clearer and deeper. I turned to move on. Near the Katahdin Lake camps we picked up a marked trail which took us to within a half mile of Moose Pond, a much easier trip than we'd done in the other direction two days earlier.

There wasn't a lot of winter climbing being done on Katahdin at that time, but interest was growing. Ranger Ralph Dolley came up with an idea and suggested to me that we might organize guided trips, furnishing food and shelter for a set charge with base camps at Roaring Brook and Russell Pond. It could be a source of winter income for both of us. During the summer, having gotten the necessary permission from Helon, we worked up a plan and had a flyer typed up covering what we planned to offer: four-, five-, or six-day snowshoe, ski, and climbing trips. A four-day, three-night trip making use of the bunkhouses would cost $42 per person, plus Park fees. We sent copies of the flyer to AMC and ATC headquarters, and hoped for business. What's that saying about best-laid plans?

That fall Dolley got an offer of a winter job in N.Y. and backed out of our proposed venture, so when I got a call from an AMC member who had a group of ten wanting to climb Katahdin in February, well, I had to do some thinking. First off, I called Ken to see if he could help me. "Happy to come along," was his quick response.

Before the snows came I started planning meals and making grocery lists, and I moved a good supply of staples in to the Roaring Brook camp. Then, faced with actual clients, I had to figure out how to get the needed fresh food in to the camp. Bob Mott and his plane came to mind as I knew he'd have skis mounted on the Piper Cub for the winter. I had become better acquainted with Bob and had flown with him a number of times since that first flight over Katahdin and the inside the Great Basin. When I explained

151

what I'd be doing, and asked him if he could fly me in to Katahdin Lake, he suggested that Sandy Stream Pond would be a lot closer for me. But, as far as we both knew, no one had ever landed a plan on the small pond. " Do you think you can do it?" I asked.

"It'll depend on the weather and the condition of the surface," he answered, more than willing to risk it. If it didn't work out, we could still use Katahdin Lake, so it seemed worth the try. My plans were coming together. The group arrived in Millinocket on a Friday night and stayed at the Great Northern Hotel, where Ken met them early Saturday morning to lead them on the ten mile snowshoe trip in to Roaring Brook. Also early that Saturday morning, Bob called me to let me know, "The temperature's 35°, and I won't fly till it warms up." Fortunately, it did climb to -20°, and we made plans to go. When I arrived at the airport, Bob informed me he would have to make two trips, one with me, and then one with the groceries.

When the engine was warmed up we took off, just me and my snowshoes, and soon we were looking down on Sandy Stream Pond, which looked awfully small with its deep covering of snow. I put my trust in Bob to make the right decision. He made a low pass to check the condition of the surface, as high windrows or ridges of snow would make it too dangerous to land. "There's one bad ridge, but I think I can land beyond it," Bob said. "Here we go," he warned banking sharply as we came in over the trees, then side-slipped that little plane down to where he could level out and set it down on the snow. As we sped toward the trees looming at the end of the pond, Bob muttered something about looking for an opening in the trees. I didn't have time to wonder if he was joking as he cut a quick turn at just the right time, bringing us to a stop not more than 75 ft. from the shore. What a great job of flying! I congratulated him on a job well done, and after watching his equally smooth takeoff, I set off for the camp at Roaring Brook to get my toboggan. I knew that hauling the boxes of food that way would be a lot easier than backpacking the half mile to the camp. I was back at the pond by the time Bob smoothly landed with my supplies, and it did not take long to move them to camp. By the time Ken and the group arrived at camp, tired and cold, the bunkhouse was warm, and I was ready to cook steaks for all.

Sunday's schedule called for a climb of South Turner Mt., but it was freezing cold and windy and only three of the group decided to climb with Ken and me. The rest settled for short nearby trips. About halfway up South Turner, two of the three with us turned back. It was rugged going, but the remaining man was determined to get to the peak, so he and Ken went ahead while I hung back and waited for them to return. When they caught up with me on the way back, they both had signs of frostbite on their noses and cheeks, so we hurried to get down out of the wind.

By Monday the wind and the temperature had moderated and the Katahdin climb was much more comfortable and enjoyable than South Turner had been the day before. With hardly a cloud in the sky you could see for miles, and everyone enjoyed the clear visibility and the panoramic views. While resting at Chimney Pond on the way down, amid talk of what a good climb and great time was had by all, some of the group decided that Ken and I deserved a break, so they would go ahead and prepare supper. Bringing up the rear we took our time, and as we reached the Basin Ponds a beautiful full moon rose from the trees directly ahead of us. So big, and it looked so close it seemed I could reach out and touch it. We stopped for a while to savor the moment, the view, and one bright star on the horizon. What a fitting end to the day. Thanks, Pamola.

Supper had been good, sleep had been deep, but now it was time to leave. The walk out on Tuesday was thankfully uneventful, and it was a happy group saying good-byes. Several of the party were already talking of coming back the next year for another climb. And they did.

The following winter, the organizer of that first group, an AMC member, got another party together including four from the previous year. As it had the previous year, the timing included Washington's Birthday. The holiday I guess made it easier for some to get away. It was an interesting group which included a Boy Scout executive, a Boston Museum of Fine Arts staff member, an

Audubon executive, I think it was three doctors, several other businessmen, and one woman, on her own, eleven in all.

When they came that year, it was the very beginning of the snowmobile era, and Elmer Woodworth who owned camps at Millinocket Lake had recently bought a Polaris machine. No more Piper Cub landing on Sandy Stream Pond, Elmer would help me get my supplies in to Roaring Brook with his new snow machine. In the early morning I drove out the newly plowed road toward the mountain to where the Park road began. Elmer had already arrived and unloaded his snowmobile. Ken and the party would follow us later.

A storm had dropped 15-16" of new snow during the night, and we had trouble right from the start. We loaded my gear on a toboggan that was to be towed behind the machine, while I was to follow on snowshoes. It didn't work out that way. First, the snowmobile bogged down in the snow, and we wound up out in front, breaking trail for the machine.

It was a cold, repetitious, tiring job. Go a ways, bog down, break trail, go some more, bog down, break trail. Finally, Elmer said he just had to give it up. We were still almost a mile from camp when he was forced to turn back and head for his truck, reluctantly leaving me to pack my supplies the rest of the way. At one point on that trek, I leaned against a tree, exhausted, wondering if I could go on. I've never been so tired. Eventually I reached the bunkhouse and got a fire going in the stove. It had been slow going for Ken and the party also, and while they were all pretty tired when they arrived, a good hearty meal soon revived everyone. Later, when I got Woodworth's bill for $12, I certainly understood. Dark had been coming on and he had been close to out of gas.

The bunkhouse had a center room with a long table, a cook stove and a sink. On each side was a good-sized room with double bunk beds, sleeping twelve people in all. On that trip I slept in the Ranger's camp, but in both places, the abundance of winter clothes and gear made it more than a little crowded. Cooking and serving meals to a group that size under those conditions proved to be quite an undertaking, but everyone was very cooperative, and gave me space to work. The woman, who confessed to being a grandmother, was a good sport, and volunteered to help wherever she could, even lugging water from the brook.

Sunday, was a day we all enjoyed, a day for relaxing and taking short trips in the area, to Sandy Stream Pond and part way up Turner Mt. Monday's Katahdin climb went well, and the group rejoiced at reaching Baxter Peak, everyone signing the register and taking pictures. Then the clouds came in and it began to snow. Oh-oh, time to head down as I well knew what this sudden change of weather could mean.

One man lost his balance and fell, sliding a ways as we were descending the Saddle Trail, but he was not hurt. While I hurried ahead to start preparations for supper, Ken stayed with the group making sure they all returned to camp safely. After a strenuous day on the Mountain and a hearty meal, not one of us was long turning in. Soon the only sounds were the crackling of the wood fire in the stove, and an occasional snore.

The packed-snow trail out to the cars made for better traveling, but ten miles on snowshoes is still a fair day's work. I'm sure there were some sore muscles in that group, a healthy tiredness to go with the good memories of their three-day wilderness experience in Baxter State Park. As for me, after expenses including Park fees, I figured a profit of about $250. Not bad for four days' work and another enjoyable winter climb for me. Ken did accept a small payment, but said he came along mainly because he loved to climb the mountain, which he did many, many times. He boasts that he has climbed Katahdin in every month of the year and all kinds of weather.

Since our trip to Arizona when I first used my new 35mm camera, I had made good use of it here at home too, carrying it with me much of the time. I had accumulated enough slides to put together a program showing the four seasons in Baxter Park, which included summer and winter climbs of Katahdin, views of many of the area's less-visited spots, and the Park's wildlife. I had many requests to show the slide program to groups in Millinocket, and always enjoyed sharing it.

Moving On

In the spring of 1960, the AMC came to me with an offer of a year-round position managing their ski lodge at Cardigan Mt. in New Hampshire. I met with the AMC management people in Boston, then took my family to see what it might be like living at Cardigan where an apartment in the lodge would be furnished. Back home, MJ and I discussed that possible change in our lives. It certainly was tempting: Year round work, no more scrounging for jobs in the winter, and what certainly appeared to be a nice place to live. Very tempting...

About that same time, Hal Dyer had begun recruiting Rangers from Baxter Park for openings in Maine's expanding State Park system, and I knew there was a good possibility that I would be in line for a Park Manager position in the near future. Years before, I had heard the call of Katahadin, we had come north, we loved Maine, and its people had been good to us. I thanked the AMC , but told them I was not interested. I was making another deal, this time with myself.

Two months later I was offered the position of Park Manager at Two Lights State Park in Cape Elizabeth. Quarters were furnished in a beautiful home overlooking the ocean with its changing tides and surf. It would be a drastic change but with our growing family, it seemed like the right next step to take. I would miss the mountains, my mountain, the woods, the moose and deer, but we knew we would go back to visit the Park and the wonderful friends we had gained in our years in the North Country.

MJ and I would be heading southward to a new job that would involve more desk work. It seemed we had come full circle in a way, but in a span of thirteen years I had experienced the challenges, the pleasures, and the trials of living in the Maine woods and gained lifelong friendships, while serving the people of Maine. I had learned a great deal about living and surviving in a different, demanding, and exciting environment, witnessed the unmatched beauty of Mt. Katahdin in all seasons, and had experienced the goodness and generosity of a wide variety of people from all walks of life. All this shared with a loving and trusting wife and our two children Eddie and Cathy whose lives had been touched also by the mountains and the woods, the spirit of Pamola, and the people of the north woods of Maine.

Eddie, Cathy, and a young friend

Epilogue

The day we arrived at our beautiful new home by the ocean, Eddie got out of the car asking, "Where are all the trees?" The view, spectacular though it was, and the house, nice as it was, did not impress my son. He missed the woods, and although I did too, I set to work getting my family settled into that large house, seven rooms in which our meager furnishings would seem lost.

I guess that living in a town such as Cape Elizabeth after our simple life of previous years brought out a hidden need to become part of a community for me and MJ.

We joined a church where MJ became a member of the Woman's Club and I got involved with the youth group. MJ was asked to join the local Garden Club, and when Eddie became a Boy Scout, I became Scout Master of the troop. The local Civil Defense organization was interested in a WW II bunker at the Park, and they asked me to take weekly geiger counter readings. Soon, contacts with the Fire Department led to my becoming a member of the newly-formed Rescue Unit. We were busy in a very different way than we ever had been upcountry, we had become part of our new community, and we had made many new friends. We were once again settling in nicely.

Eddie was ten and Cathy seven when we moved to Cape Elizabeth and the transition was perhaps more difficult for them than it was for MJ and me. More affluent surroundings and a larger school were a challenging contrast to the small school and mill children they'd known in Millinocket, and they were a long time adjusting.

Construction crews were just beginning work on the new park I would supervise and my first year on the job was spent coordinating the work with park engineers in Augusta, while also making friends with Park neighbors, some of whom were not happy that they would have a State Park next door. The dedication of the completed Two Lights State Park took place the following June and a few years later the adjoining Crescent Beach Park was opened. Work and life beside the every-changing sea in southern Maine were going well, although the mountains and woods of the north were never far from my thoughts. And, MJ and I made regular trips to Katahdin with Eddie and Cathy until long after they reached adulthood.

Not long after my Park work settled down, word reached me that a terrific October snowstorm up north had trapped a woman climber on Mt. Katahdin and had also trapped Ranger Ralph Heath who had tried to rescue her. Katahdin called me again. I joined the search parties in a futile attempt to locate them until the search was called off. Their bodies were found the following spring. Why did Pamola keep entering my thoughts?

During that time, the Maine State Park System continued to grow and in 1968, six districts were formed, and I was named Supervisor of a southern district. That meant we had to buy a house of our own in the area, and we found one we liked in North Saco. The years passed, and after completing 36 years as a Maine State employee, I retired in 1982. MJ and I looked forward to a new freedom. Eddie and Cathy were grown by then and busy establishing their own families, so we were free to travel around the country which we did, even to Bermuda which we enjoyed.

Besides our travels, MJ enjoyed each of the grandchildren as they came along but increasingly, MJ's health had become a concern. She began to have serious medical problems and shortly after her 70th birthday and our 50th wedding anniversary, she passed away. I had lost my love, my friend, my partner. I was alone with my memories of our long shared life.

About a year later, while passing through Damariscotta, I stopped to call on Jake Day's widow, Martha, or "Perk" as Jake always called her. We had kept in touch with the Days mainly though Christmas cards, and I had in mind to buy a Jake Day painting of the North Country, maybe of Katahdin if one was available. No answer when I rang the doorbell, so I left a note. That led to an invitation to lunch, then a date for dinner out. Martha and I had both found a new love, and we exchanged vows at her church in Damariscotta where we planned to live. In time we built a house on two wooded acres on Duck Puddle Pond, not far from Damariscotta. While there is no mountain in view, we have birds, wildlife, and good fishing right at hand, and a sign at the head of the driveway reads "WERLERS' WOODS."

I have kept busy as a member of the Pemaquid River Association, and I am active with Friends of Maine State Parks. One big project I've enjoyed working on over the past year or so has been making plaques for all of Maine's state parks and memorials. Each plaque starts with a slate outline of the state mounted on cedar, then on the individual plaques, the specific park or memorial is marked, and the names of the mangers for that location are listed.

I've also spent many hours over the last few years, helping to catalog Jake's many photos and caring forsome of his paintings, so many of which represent the richest parts of both my life and Martha's back through the years. And Martha and I have continued to return to Baxter State Park every year and each time, it has felt like coming home.

Eventually I know that Martha will lie beside Jake in Damariscotta while MJ and I will go home together to Daicey Mt. where our ashes will be scattered. We'll see the sun rise each day on our beloved mountain, and hear once again the call of Katahdin. Perhaps our grandchildren and even their children will hear that call too.

Order Form

Have you enjoyed *The Call of Katahdin*?
Perhaps your friends and family would too!
Send your order to:

The Call of Katahdin
Cranberry Knoll Publishers, LLC
P.O. Box 1317
Yarmouth, ME 04096

Please send me ____ copies of **The Call of Katahdin** at $14.95 per copy plus $3.00 each for postage and handling. Maine residents, please add 5% sales tax.

Enclosed is my check for $ _____

Send to _____

Street _____

City _____ State _____ ZIP Code _____

The Call of Katahdin
Cranberry Knoll Publishers, LLC
P.O. Box 1317
Yarmouth, ME 04096

Please send me ____ copies of **The Call of Katahdin** at $14.95 per copy plus $3.00 each for postage and handling. Maine residents, please add 5% sales tax.

Enclosed is my check for $ _____

Send to _____

Street _____

City _____ State _____ ZIP Code _____